CHRISTMAS SPIRIT

CHRISTMAS SPIRIT

The Joyous Stories, Carols, Feasts,

and Traditions of the Season

GREGORY WILBUR & GEORGE GRANT

Cumberland House

NASHVILLE, TENNESSEE

Published by Cumberland House Publishing, Inc., 431 Harding Industrial Drive, Nashville, Tennessee 37211.

Jacket design by Tonya Presley

Library of Congress Cataloging-in-Publication Data

Wilbur, Gregory,
    Christmas spirit : the joyous stories, carols, feasts, and traditions of the season / Gregory Wilbur & George Grant.
      p.   cm.
    Includes index.
    ISBN 1-58182-204-9 (alk. paper)
    1. Christmas. 2. Carols, English—Texts. I. Grant, George, 1954– II. Title.
GT4985.W497 1999
394.2663—dc21

                          99-043363

Printed in the United States of America
2 3 4 5 6 7 8 9 10 — 05 04 03 02 01

To Our Beloved Wives
Sophia and Karen

CONTENTS

ACKNOWLEDGMENTS

It is in the old Christmas carols, hymns, and traditions—those which date from the Middle Ages—that we find not only what makes Christmas poetic and soothing and stately, but first and foremost what makes Christmas exciting. The exciting quality of Christmas rests on an ancient and admitted paradox. It rests upon the paradox that the power and center of the whole universe may be found in some seemingly small matter, that the stars in their courses may move like a moving wheel around the neglected outhouse of an inn.
G. K. CHESTERTON (1874–1936)

As we undertook the task of writing, editing, compiling, and anthologizing the sundry pieces in the book, we had far more than sugar plums dancing in our heads; we also had the fond remembrances of innumerable Christmases past and the cherished memories of each of the dear people who made them so wondrous for us. As a result we were able to realize anew the marvelous truth of Chesterton's truism—that the spirit of Christmas is a paradox precisely because its largeness is made manifest in the smallest of ways: in little kindnesses, tiny pleasures, and obscure delights among ordinary people in the simplest of circumstances.

Our parents, our brothers and sisters, our spouses and children, our friends and co-workers, and our students have celebrated this amazing reality with us over the years; and to each of them we are grateful. You gave us our holiday traditions and made our Christmases invariably merry.

The good folks at Cumberland House, and particularly our friends Ron and Julia Pitkin, embraced our vision for books that are distinctly practical, down-to-earth, fun, historically informed, non-didactic, and yet fully within the parameters of a Christian worldview. They have given us the extraordinary gift of a refreshing publishing experience.

The soundtrack for this project—in other words, the music we were listening to as we wrote—was provided by the appropriately disparate scores of William Coulter, The Baltimore Consort, Anuna, Jessye Norman, Barry and Shelly Phillips, David Diamond, and G.F. Handel. Likewise, the midnight musings—in other words, the books we were reading as we wrote—were provided by the equally diverse prose of J.R.R. Tolkien, Thomas Chalmers, Jan Karon, G.K. Chesterton, Dorothy Sayers, James Blaylock, Abraham Kuyper. Their influence, we hope, is obvious in both content and form.

As always though, it was our beloved wives, Sophia and Karen who most enabled us to write this very personal exploration of the joyous stories, carols, feasts, and traditions of the Christmas season. With nary a complaint, they sacrificed many a weekend as we struggled to squeeze some writing into an already too hectic schedule. They epitomize for us the Christmas spirit day in and day out throughout the entire year.

SUMMER 1999
Bannockburn College

INTRODUCTION

For some of us, reading is a required tradition during the Christmas season. I don't mean ordinary books that we catch up on during the holiday vacation. Rather, we long for an ambience that evokes that timeless sense of magic and holiness that is often called "the spirit of Christmas." Of course we need to reread the nativity story to savor its pure essence. Yet we hunger for more. With nearly two thousand Christmases behind us, nostalgia must be satiated.
JAMES S. BELL (1952–)

Christmas is nearly everyone's favorite time of year because it is adorned with so many special celebrations, happy memories, delightful stories, wonderful songs, and rich recipes. It is a season of selfless giving, expressive love, and poetic joy. It is a time for family togetherness, for snuggling up to the hearthside, for recalling legends and fables, and for celebrating the things that matter most. As a result, Christmas has been the focus of some of the greatest art, music, literature, and ideas of all time.

While many of the richest and most satisfying aspects of the season have passed into common practice, their meaning and significance have often been shrouded in forgetfulness, neglect, ignorance, superstition, or misunderstanding. Alas, this has meant that their greatest pungency, power, and purpose has been lost to us.

This anthology is an attempt to recapture the delectable essence of the season by gathering together in one place a sampling of all those elements which contribute to the joyous spirit of Christmas—from the origins of our most cherished holiday traditions, observances, and rituals to the observations of the wisest men and women of the ages on their essential meaning and significance. Here are all the whys and wherefores of mistletoe, plum pudding, holly and ivy, Advent wreaths, nativity scenes, caroling, sleigh rides, Christmas trees, jingle bells, Pascha, wassailing, Twelfth Night, twinkling lights, Noel, gift giving, and Saint Nick.

Each chapter profiles a particular aspect of the holiday season—which moves from the preparation of Advent, the celebration of Christmastide, and the reflection of Epiphany—and some of the great stories, carols, feasts, and traditions that, to our minds at least, best exemplifies its essential spirit. The poetry, epigrams, quotations, and excerpts are not merely anthologized illustrations. They are instead definitive—of both the season and the spirit.

Our aim is to reassert the substantiveness of our celebrations. It is to recover meaning. It is to revitalize our holidays by reviving their truest intent and deepest significance. Ours is a desire for a rediscovery of the profound joy of the "Christmas Spirit" rather than mere visceral pleasure of the "happy holidays."

Admittedly this kind of book bears the inevitable stamp of subjective experience. In fact, it is a companion volume to a series of books published by Cumberland House designed to exposit some very personal perspectives of some very personal passions. *Letters Home* deals with the sage counsel of bygone days, *Best Friends* explores the ways friendship shapes our lives, *Just Visiting* takes a look at the way travel has enlightened lives and viewpoints throughout history, *Lost Causes* discusses seemingly vanquished, yet always resolute convictions, *Shelf Life* examines the bookish life and all its compliments, *Garden Graces* deals with the joys of the soil and its fruits, and *Sports Fan* delves into the peculiar pleasures competition and games afford us. Yet to come are additional volumes on domesticity, music, handicrafts, architecture, food, and Eastertide.

By its very nature, this book—like all the others in the series—is more a testimony than a documentary. These are our passions, our traditions, and our sundry favorites. Our purpose in writing then, is to both express and profess. And so we do.

CHRISTMAS SPIRIT

Yuletide

*T*he holiday season—what we generally just call Christmastime—is actually a long sequence of holy days, festal revelries, and liturgical rites that are collectively known as Yuletide. Beginning with Advent, a time of preparation and repentance, proceeding to Christmas, a time of celebration and generosity, and concluding with Epiphany, a time of remembrance and thanksgiving, Yuletide traditions enable us to see out the old year with faith and love while ushering in the new year with hope and joy. It is a season fraught with meaning and significance. Unfortunately, it is also such a busy season that its meaning and significance can all too easily be obscured either by well-intended materialistic pursuits—frenzied shopping trips to the mall to find just the right Christmas gift—or by the less benign demands, desires, wants, and needs that are little more than grist for human greed. The traditions of Yuletide were intended to guard us against such things—and thus, are actually more relevant today than ever before.

When I think of Christmas Eves, Christmas feasts, Christmas songs, and Christmas stories, I know that they do not represent a short and transient gladness. Instead, they speak of a joy unspeakable and full of glory. God love the world and sent His Son. Whosoever believes in Him will not perish, but have everlasting life. That is Christmas joy. That is the Christmas spirit.

Corrie ten Boom (1892–1983)

There is something about saying, "We always do this," which helps keep the years together. Time is such an elusive thing that if we keep on meaning to do something interesting, but never do it, year would follow year with no special thoughtfulness being expressed in making gifts, surprises, charming table settings, and familiar, favorite food. Tradition is a good gift intended to guard the best gifts.

Edith Schaeffer (1916–)

In Bethlehem, that noble place,
As by prophecy said it was,
Of the virgin Mary, full of grace,
Salvator mundi natus est. *

On Christmas night an angel it told
To the shepherds keeping their fold,
That in Bethlehem with beastés wold,
Salvator mundi natus est.

The shepherdés were compassed right
About them was a great light:
"Dread ye nought," said the angel bright,
Salvator mundi natus est.

"Behold to you we bring great joy,
For why, Jesus is born this day;
To us of Mary, that mildé may,
Salvator mundi natus est.

"And thus in faith find it ye shall,
Lying poorly in an ox's stall."
The shepherds then lauded God all,
Quia Salvator mundi natus est.
⊷ *Medieval Carol (c. 1400)* ⊶

* Today the savior is born.

A contempt of the monuments and the wisdom of the past, may be justly reckoned one of the reigning follies of these days, to which pride and idleness have equally contributed.

⊸ Samuel Johnson (1709–1784) ⊷

To comprehend the history of a thing is to unlock the mysteries of its present, and more, to disclose the profundities of its future.

⊸ Hilaire Belloc (1870–1953) ⊷

Why does the chilling winter's morn
Smile like a field beset with corn;
Or smell to a mead new-shorn,
Thus on the sudden? Come and see
The cause why things thus fragrant be:

'Tis he is born, whose quickening birth
Gives life and lustre, public mirth,
To heaven and the under-earth.

We see him come, and know him ours,
Who, with his sunshine and his showers,
Turns all the patient ground to flowers.

⊸ Robert Herrick (1591–1674) ⊷

Custom reconciles us to everything.
Edmund Burke (1729–1797)

Those who are in rebellion against memory are the ones who wish to live without knowledge.
Richard Weaver (1910–1963)

I love her to tears, at sight, from the first,
As she comes from the woods,
In storm and snow.
So awkward her branches, the shyest of firs!
We fashion her threads unhurriedly, slow.
Her garments of silvery gossamer lace,
Patterns of tinsel, and spangles aglow
From branch to branch down to the base.
Boris Pasternak (1890–1960)

Somehow not only for Christmas
But all the long year through,
The joy that you give to others
Is the joy that comes back to you.
And the more you spend in blessing
The poor and lonely and sad,
The more of your heart's possessing
Returns to make you glad.
John Greenleaf Whittier (1807–1892)

Are you willing to believe that the
Blessed life which began in Bethlehem
Nineteen hundred years ago is the image
And brightness of the Eternal Love?
Then you can keep Christmas. And if
You keep it for a day, why not always?
But you can never keep it alone.
Henry van Dyke (1852–1933)

Blessed babe! What glorious features
Spotless fair, divinely bright!
Must He dwell with brutal creatures?
How could angels bear the sight?
Was there nothing but a manger
Cursed sinners could afford
To receive the Heavenly Stranger?
Did they thus affront their Lord?
Yet may'st thou live to know and fear Him,
He who deigned to incarnate earth's days;
So go and dwell forever near Him,
See His face, and sing His praise.

Isaac Watts (1674–1748)

On this day earth shall ring
With the song children sing
To the Lord, Christ our King,
Born on earth to save us;
Him the Father gave us.
Ideo, Ideo,
Ideo gloria in excelsis Deo!

Charlemagne the Great (742–814)

On a winter's night long, long ago
The bells ring loud and the bells ring low,
When high howled wind, and down fell snow.
Carillon, carilla
Saint Joseph, he and Nostre Dame,
Riding on an ass, full weary came
From Nazareth into Bethlehem.
And the small child Jesus smile on you.

And Bethlehem inn they stood before
The bells ring loud and the bells ring more,
The landlord bade them begone from his door
Carillon, carilla
"Poor folk" says he, "must lie where they may,
For the Duke of Jewry comes this way,
With all his train on a Christmas Day."
And the small child Jesus smile on you.

Poor folk that may my carol hear
The bells ring loud and the bells ring clear,
See! God's one child had hardest cheer!
Carillon, carilla.
Men grown hard on Christmas morn;
The dumb beast by and a babe forlorn.
It was very, very cold when our Lord was born
And the small child Jesus smile on you.

Now these were Jews as Jews must be
The bells ring loud and the bells ring clear,
But Christian men in a band are we
Carillon, carilla.
Empty we go, and ill be-dight,
Singing Noel on a winter's night.
Give us to sup by the warm firelight,
And the small child Jesus smile on you.

Hilaire Belloc (1870–1953)

Christmas is coming; the goose is getting fat;
Please put a penny in the old man's hat;
Jesus would have us celebrate—just like that.
Charles Dickens (1812–1870)

Intelligent children, whether they believed or not in the sacred and benevolent burglary every Christmas Eve, would feel that the magi, the saint, and the heathen god did not really make up the image of the old man with the furred coat and the reindeers: or if they did not feel so, they would have developed their intelligence at the ruinous expense of their childhood. But indeed, in such cases, childhood and intelligence fail together.
G. K. Chesterton (1874–1936)

All heaven and earth resound with that subtle and delicately balanced truth that the old paths are the best paths after all.

J. C. Ryle (1816–1900)

Every tradition grows ever more venerable—the more remote its origin, the more confused that origin is. The reverence due to it increases from generation to generation. The tradition finally becomes holy and inspires awe. Is this ill or fine? If the accumulated wisdom and the tested habits of the ages accounts for naught, then surely it is ill. But if such things afford security and sanity, then it is an augur of great good. Sense and sensibility should sway us toward the confident latter and not the impetuous former.

James Gleason Archer (1844–1909)

Christ took our nature on him, not that he
'Bove all things loved it, for the purity:
No, but he dressed him with our human trim,
Because our flesh stood most in need of him.

Robert Herrick (1591–1674)

True contentment is a thing as active as agriculture. It is the power of getting out of any situation all that there is in it. It is arduous and it is rare. It is the discipline of Epiphany.

G. K. Chesterton (1874–1936)

Maker of the sun, He is made under the sun. In the Father He remains, from His mother He goes forth. Creator of heaven and earth, He was born on earth under heaven. Unspeakably wise, He is wisely speechless. Filling the world, He lies in a manger. Ruler of the stars, He nurses at His mother's bosom. He is both great in the nature of God, and small in the form of a servant.

Augustine (354–430)

Come, lovely Name; life of our hope!
Lo, we hold our hearts wide ope!
Unlock thy cabinet of day,
Dearest Sweet, and come away.
Lo, how the thirsty lands
Gasp for thy golden showers, with long-stretched hands!
Lo, how the labouring earth
That hopes to be
All heaven by thee,
Leaps at thy birth!

Come, royal Name; and pay the expense
Of all this precious patïence;
O come away,
And kill the death of this delay.
O see so many worlds of barren years
Melted and measured out in seas of tears.
O see the weary lids of wakeful hope
(Love's eastern windows) all wide ope
With curtain drawn,
To catch the day-break of thy dawn.

Richard Crashaw (c.1613–1649)

You have come to us as a small child, but you have brought us the greatest of all gifts, the gift of eternal love. Caress us with your tiny hands, embrace us with your tiny arms, and pierce our hearts with your soft, sweet cries.

Bernard of Clairvaux (1090–1153)

Neither in halls nor yet in bowers
Born would he not be,
Neither in castles nor yet in towers
That seemly were to see;
But at his Father's will
The prophecy to fulfill,
Betwixt an ox and an ass
Jesus, this king, born he was.
Heavén he bring us till!

Coventry Mystery Play (c. 1200)

The Son of God became a man to enable men to become the sons of God.

⊶ *C. S. Lewis (1898–1963)* ⊷

The true Christian religion is incarnational and thus does not begin at the top, as all other religions do; it begins at the bottom. You must run directly to the manger and the mother's womb, embrace the Infant and Virgin's Child in your arms and look at Him—born, being nursed, growing up, going about in human society, teaching, dying, rising again, ascending above all the heavens, and having authority over all things.

⊶ *Martin Luther (1483–1546)* ⊷

The antiquary of tradition is the preserver of all that is right and good and true. It is the wisest and most progressive of all the human impulses—for it guarantees continuity for the uncertain days of the future. Let every man and woman warmly embrace the lessons of the past.

Calvin Coolidge (1872–1933)

When love of us called him to see
If we'd vouchsafe his company,
He left his Father's court, and came
Lightly as a lambent flame,
Leaping upon the hills, to be
The humble King of you and me.

Richard Crashaw (c.1613–1649)

Hail to the King of Bethlehem
Who weareth in His diadem
The yellow crocus for the gem
Of His authority.

Henry W. Longfellow (1807–1882)

G. K. Chesterton and the Joy of Celebration

Weak things must boast of being new, like so many new German philosophies. But strong things can boast of being old. Strong things can boast of being moribund.

G. K. Chesterton (1874–1936)

Gilbert Keith Chesterton was surely among the brightest minds of the twentieth century—a prolific journalist, best-selling novelist, insightful poet, popular debater, astute literary critic, grassroots reformer, and profound humorist. Recognized by friend and foe alike as one of the most perspicacious, epigrammatic, and jocose prose stylists in the entire literary canon, he is today the most quoted writer in the English language besides William Shakespeare.

His remarkable output of books—more than a hundred published in his lifetime and half again that many afterward—covered an astonishing array of subjects from economics, art, history, biography, and social criticism to poetry, detective stories, philosophy, travel, and religion. His most amazing feat was not merely his vast output or wide range but the consistency and clarity of his thought, his uncanny ability to tie everything together. In the heart of nearly every paragraph he wrote was a jaw-dropping aphorism or a mind-boggling paradox that left readers shaking their heads in bemusement and wonder.

But Chesterton was not only a prodigious creator of characters, he was also a prodigious character in his own right. At over six feet and three hundred pounds his romantically rumpled appearance—often enhanced with the flourish of a cape and a swordstick—made him appear as nearly enigmatic, anachronistic, and convivial as he actually was. Perhaps that was a part of the reason why he was one of the most beloved men of his time—even his ideological opponents regarded him with great affection. His humility, his wonder at existence, his graciousness and his sheer sense of joy set him apart not only from most of the artists and celebrities during the first half of the twentieth century, but from most anyone and everyone.

He was amazingly prescient—alas, all too many of the very things he predicted have come to pass: the mindless faddism of pop culture, the rampant materialism permeating society, the moral relativism subsuming age-old ethical standards, disdain of religion, the unfettered censorship by the press (as opposed to censorship of the press), the grotesque uglification of the arts, the rise of the twin evils of monolithic business and messianic government with the accompanying results of wage slavery and the loss of individual liberty. It seems that on nearly every subject, Chesterton's words ring truer today than when they were first written nearly a century ago.

But perhaps the most remarkable thing about Chesterton was not his prodigious literary output, his enormous popularity, or his cultural sagacity. Instead, it was his enormous capacity to love—to love people, to love the world around him, and to love life. His all-encompassing love was especially evident at Christmastime.

Maisie Ward, Chesterton's authoritative biographer and friend asserted, "Some men, it may be, are best moved to reform by hate, but Chesterton was best moved by love and nowhere does that love shine more clearly than in all he wrote about Christmas." Indeed, he wrote a great deal about Christmas throughout his life—and as a result his love shines abroad even now, nearly three-quarters of a century after his death. He wrote scintillating Christmas essays, poignant Christmas verse, and adventurous Christmas stories. He wrote Christmas reviews, editorials, satires, and expositions. He wrote of Christmas recipes and Christmas presents and Christmas sermons. They all bespeak the stalwart faith, the abiding hope, and the infectious joy he drew from the celebration of Christ's incarnation.

Some of his more cosmopolitan contemporaries believed that his child-like glee in Christmas confirmed their suspicions that he was somehow stunted emotionally—that his irrepressible fixation on the Yuletide Spirit was evidence of the immaturity of his faith. But Chesterton would have none of that. He said, "Most sensible people say that adults cannot be expected to appreciate Christmas as much as children appreciate it. But I am not sure that even sensible people are always right; and this has been my principle reason for deciding to be silly—a decision that is now irrevocable. It may be because I am silly, but I rather think that, relatively to the rest of the year, I enjoy Christmas more than I did when I was a child. My faith demands that such be the case. The more mature I become the more I need to embrace the joys of the incarnation. The more mature I become, the more I need to be but a child."

Of course, there was more to Chesterton's love of Yuletide than merely fun and games, food and gifts, festivity and gaiety. He seemed almost intuitively to grasp the fact that the keeping of times and seasons throughout the year was an essential Christian discipline—the discipline of sanctifying time. It may seem to us an overly simplified notion, but he realized that he needed to walk in Christian traditions in order to fully walk in the Christian tradition.

Virtually, every Biblical injunction about the use of time underlines the importance of each moment that passes. Christians are admonished to make the most of their time (Ephesians 5:15). They are to redeem the time (Colossians 4:5). They are to utilize every day to the utmost (Hebrews

3:13). In short, they are to sanctify the time (Ecclesiastes 3:1-8). According to the Bible, a believer's time is not his or her own. It is not theirs to dispose of as they might choose. They have been bought with a price (1 Corinthians 6:20). Therefore they are to set our days, weeks, and years apart to the Lord for His glory (Romans 14:6-12).

In the Old Testament, the days were therefore carefully divided into eight distinct periods: dawn, morning, midday, dark, evening, and three night watches. These were distinguished in the lives of believers by times and seasons of prayer (Psalm 55:17; Daniel 6:10). In the New Testament, the value of this kind of liturgical clock was affirmed by the followers of Christ who punctuated and accentuated their urgent task of evangelization with the discipline of regular spiritual refreshment (Acts 3:1).

Similarly, the weeks of God's people were ordered with purposeful sanctity. In the Old Testament, the week centered around the Sabbath and the attendant sacrifices. In the New Testament, the week revolved around the Lord's day and the sacraments. Thus, each week had its own pace, its own schedule, its own priorities, and its own order. Thus, believers were able to give form to function and function to form (Deuteronomy 5:12; Hebrews 10:24-25). The liturgical calendar enabled them to wait on the Lord and thus to run and not be weary and to walk and not be faint (Isaiah 40:31).

Even the years were given special structure and significance to reinforce the Biblical conception of the stewardship of time. In ancient Israel, feasts, fasts, and festivals paced the community of faith in its progression through the months (Exodus 13:6-10; Psalm 31:15). The early church continued this stewardship of time, punctuating the years with liturgical seasons—with Lent, Easter, Ascension, Pentecost, and the Yuletide celebrations of Advent, Christmas, and Epiphany. Thus, God's people were continually enabled and equipped to run the race (Philippians 2:16), to fight the fight

(Ephesians 6:10-18), to finish the course (2 Timothy 4:7), and to keep the faith (2 Timothy 3:10).

For Chesterton, the momentous medieval conversion of the old pagan European tribes—the Lombards, Celts, Burgundians, Goths, Saxons, Franks, Huns, Normans, Jutes, and Teutons—meant not only the conversion of individuals and families but of whole cultures. As a result, the long-held traditions and rituals of their calendars were ultimately as transformed by the Gospel as were the long-held habits and inclinations of their hearts. Their ancient pagan winter festivals were thus subsumed into the new celebrations of the Christian year. That understanding made Chesterton impatient with those—either from within or from without the Church—who criticized Christmas for being somehow less than Christian.

He wrote, "There is one very vile habit that the pedants have, and that is explaining to a man why he does a thing which the man himself can explain quite well—and quite differently. If I go down on all-fours to find a penny, it annoys me to be told by a passing biologist that I am really doing it because my remote ancestors were quadrupeds. I concede that he knows all about biology, or even a great deal about my ancestors; but I know he is wrong, because he does not know about the penny. If I climb a tree after a stray cat, I am unconvinced when a stray anthropologist tells me that I am doing it because I am essentially arboreal and barbaric. I happen to know why I am doing it; and I know it is because I am amiable and somewhat over-civilized. Scientists will talk to a man on general guesswork about things they know no more about than about his pocket money or his pet cat. Religion is one of them, and all the festivals and formalities that are rooted in religion. Thus a man will tell me that in keeping Christmas I am not keeping a Christian feast, but a pagan feast. That is exactly as if he told me that I was not feeling furiously angry, but only a little sad. I know how I am feeling, all right; and why I am feeling it. I know this in the case of cats, pennies, anger, and Christmas Day."

For him, Christmas joy was undiminished by either the materialists who wished to over-commercialize the celebration or the methodologists who wished to over-rationalize it. Instead, Chesterton embraced Yuletide traditions and the thundering truth that they inevitably teach us—often over and against all world-wisdom. Thus, he wrote, "Christmas and health are commonly in some antagonism, and I, for one, am heartily on the side of Christmas. Glancing down a newspaper column I see the following alarming sentence: 'The Lancet adds a frightful corollary that the only way to eat Christmas pudding with perfect impunity is to eat it alone.' At first the meaning of this sentence deceived me. I thought it meant that the eater of Christmas pudding must be in a state of sacred isolation like an anchorite at prayer. I thought it meant that the presence of one's fellow creatures in some way disturbed the subtle nervous and digestive process through which Christmas pudding was beneficent. It sounded rather mad and wicked, certainly; but not madder or more wicked than many other things that I have read in scientific journals. But on rereading the passage, I see that my first impression did the Lancet an injustice. The sentence really means that when one eats a Christmas pudding one should eat nothing but Christmas pudding. 'It is,' says the Lancet, 'a complete meal in itself.' This is, I should say, a question of natural capacity, not to say of cubic capacity. I know a kind of person who would find one Christmas pudding a complete meal in itself, and even a little over. For my own part, I should say that three or perhaps four, Christmas puddings might be said to constitute a complete meal in themselves. But in any case, this sudden conversion of science to plum pudding is a fine example of the fickleness of the human intellect and the steadiness of the human appetite. Scientific theories change, but the plum pudding remains the same, century after century (I do not mean the individual pudding of course, but the type), a permanent monument of human mysticism and human mirth."

For him, the commemoration of history's most glorious advent, incarnation, and epiphany called for a radical kind of rearrangement of life that fully reflected its true import. Thus, Chesterton celebrated. He celebrated by embracing Yuletide traditions with zealous mirth and with all ardent exultation. It was after all, both his confession and his profession that Jesus Christ is not just the hinge upon which creation turns, He is its very raison d'être. Therefore anything other than a very merry Christmas, it seemed, was not only a suppression of joy, it was also a breach of faith.

When at this season of the year we wish our friends a "Merry Christmas," it is essential to realize that true merriment of the heart is contingent upon the recognition of the truth that Christ was born in Bethlehem for our salvation. The word "merry" is from an old Anglo-Saxon word that sometimes meant "famous," "illustrious," "great," or "mighty." Originally, to be merry did not imply to be merely mirthful, but strong and gallant. It was in this sense that gallant soldiers were called "merry men." Favorable weather was called "merry weather." Brisk winds were called a "merry gale." Spenser speaks of London as "merry London." The word "merry" carries with it the double thought of "might" and "mirth," and is used both ways in Scripture. One of the early Christmas carols was "God Rest Ye Merry Gentlemen." The Christian is to engage in spiritual merriment as he thinks upon the fact that, through the redemption, he becomes a child of God's family. The Bible teaches that the angels made merry at Christ's birth.

Billy Graham (1918–)

YULETIDE GREETINGS

Een Plesierige Kerfees	Afrikaans
Schenorhavor Dzenount	Armenian
Chestita Koleda	Bulgarian
Felices Pascuas	Catalonian
Srecan Bozic	Croatian
Vesele Vanoce	Czech
Glaedelig Jul	Danish
Zalig Kerstfeest	Dutch
Merry Christmas	English
Roomsaid Joulu Puhi	Estonian
Idah Saidan Wa Sanah Jadidah	Farsi
Hauskaa Joulu	Finnish
Vrolijke Kerstmis	Flemish
Joyeux Noel	French
Nodlaig Nait Cugat	Gaelic
Frohliche Weihnachten	German
Boldog Karacsony	Hungarian
Buon Natale	Italian
Meri Kurisumasu	Japanese
Kung His Hsin Nien	Mandarin
Gledelig Jul	Norwegian
Boas Festas	Portuguese
Sarbatori Vesele	Romanian
Hristos se Rodi	Serbian

Feliz Navidad	Spanish
Glad Jul	Swedish
Bing Chu Shen Tan	Tuan
Noeliniz Ve Yeni Yiliniz Kutlu Olsun	Turkish
Chrystos Rozdzajetsia Slawyte Jeho	Ukranian
Nadolig Llawen	Welsh

Advent

Advent is a season of preparation. For centuries Christians have used the month prior to the celebration of Christ's incarnation to ready their hearts and their homes for the great festival. While we moderns tend to do a good bit of bustling about in the crowded hours between Thanksgiving and Christmas—shopping for presents, compiling guest lists, mailing holiday greeting cards, perusing catalogs, decorating hearth and home, baking favorite confections, and getting ready for one party after another—that hardly constitutes the kind of preparation Advent calls for. Indeed, traditionally Advent has been a time of quiet introspection, personal examination, and repentance. A time to slow down, to take stock of the things that matter the most, and to do a thorough inner housecleaning. Advent is, as the ancient dogma of the Church asserts, a Little Pascha—a time of fasting, prayer, confession, and reconciliation. All the great Advent stories, hymns, customs, and rituals—from the medieval liturgical antiphons and Scrooge's A Christmas Carol *to the lighting of Advent candles and the eating of Martinmas beef are attuned to this notion: the best way to prepare for the coming of the Lord is to make straight His pathway in our hearts.*

Loud rings the warning voice around,
And earth's dark places hear the sound;
Away false dreams; vain shadows, fly;
Lo! Christ, the Dayspring, shines on high.
Anonymous Latin Hymn Writer, c. 900

The pitch of the stall was glorious
Though the straw was dusty and old
The wind sang with orchestral beauty
Though it blew bitter and cold

The night was mysteriously gleaming
Though the earth was fallen, forlorn
For under the eaves of splendor
A child-The Child-was born

Oxen Sheep and doves
Crowded round Nativity's scene
Though the world still failed to grasp
T'was here that peace had been

Cast out into a cave
When no room was found for Him
His coming was a scourge
That cleansed a robber's den

While the Temple's become a cattle stall
Where beasts and such are sold
The Child's turned Manger into Temple
And changed the base to gold

Tis the paradox of the ages:
Worldly wisdom will ne're relent
To notice signs of visitation
Nor the cords of the whip of Advent

❧ *Tristan Gylberd (1954–)* ☙

How proper it is that Christmas should follow Advent. For him who looks toward the future, the manger is situated on Golgotha, and the cross has already been raised in Bethlehem.

❧ *Dag Hammarskjold (1905–1961)* ☙

Over the apple-tress wit their red load
In world's-end orchards, over dark yew woods,
O'er fires of sunset glassed in wizard streams,
O'er mill and meadow of those farthest lands,
Over the reapers, over the sere sails
Of homing ships and every breaking wave,
Over the haven and the entrancéd town,
O'er hearths aflame with fir-trunks and fir-cones,
Over the children playing in the streets,
Over the harpers harping on the bridge,
O'er the lovers in their dream and their desire,
There falls from the high heaven a subtle sense
Of presage and a deep, expectant hush,
And the wise watchers know the time draws on
And that amid the snows of that same year
The earth will bear her longed-for perfect Fruit.

Richard Lawson Gales (1871–1932)

Advent Carols and Hymns

The Great Advent Antiphons
c. 6th or 7th century

The *Great Advent Antiphons* are also known as the *O Antiphons* because they all begin with the word "O." An antiphon is a chant, usually in Latin, that was sung before the singing of a psalm or canticle (a song sung by someone in Scripture). The following medieval antiphons, reserved for the last week of Advent, introduced the singing of the *Magnificat* (Mary's Song) during vespers. These evening services included a cantor (lead chanter) who would sing one of these texts before leading everyone in singing the Virgin Mary's canticle, the *Magnificat.* This is also where the concept of antiphonal singing comes from with two or more groups singing alternating lines of a song. In fact, the word antiphon originates from a Greek word that means "resonating with." This particular set of antiphons provided the source material for the great Advent hymn *O Come, O Come, Emmanuel.*

O Sapientia
December 16
O, Wisdom, which camest out of the mouth of the most high,
And reachest from one end to another,
Mightily and sweetly ordering all things:
Come and teach us the way of prudence.

O Adonai
December 17
O, Adonai and Leader of the house of Israel,
Who appearedst in the bush to Moses in a flame of fire,
And gavest him the Law in Sinai:
Come and deliver us with outstretched arm.

O Radix Jesse
December 18
O, Root of Jesse, which standest for an ensign of the people,
At whom kings shall shut their mouths,
To whom Gentiles shall seek:
Come and deliver us, and tarry not.

O Clavis David
December 19
O, Key of David and Sceptre of the house of Israel;
That openest, and no man shutteth; and shuttest, and no man openeth:
Come and bring the prisoner out of the prison-house,
And him that sitteth in darkness, and the shadow of death.

O Oriens
December 20
O, Dayspring, Brightness of Light everlasting,
And Sun of Righteousness:
Come and enlighten him that sitteth in darkness, and the shadow of death.

O Rex gentium
December 21
O, King of the nations, and their Desire;
The Cornerstone, who makest both one:
Come and save mankind, whom thou formedst of clay.

O Emmanuel
December 22
O, Emmanuel, our King and Lawgiver,
The Desire of all nations, and their Salvation:
Come and save us, O Lord our God.

O Virgo virginum
December 23
O, Virgin of virgins, how shall this be?
For neither before thee was any like thee, nor shall there be after.
Daughters of Jerusalem, why marvel ye at me?
The thing which ye behold is a divine mystery.

MAGNIFICAT
Mary's Song
Luke 2:46-55
The Magnificat, known as Mary's song from the Gospel of Luke, is a beautiful expression of praise sung by Mary in response to her cousin Elizabeth's greeting. Elizabeth, who was at the time miraculously pregnant with John the Baptist, declared that at the moment of hearing Mary's voice, the infant

leapt for joy in her womb. "And blessed is she that believed, for there shall be a fulfillment of those things which were told her from the Lord." Luke 1:45

My soul doth magnify the Lord:
And my spirit hath rejoiced in God my Saviour.
    For he hath regarded the lowliness of his handmaiden.
For behold from henceforth,
    All generations shall call me blessed.
For he that is mighty hath magnified me,
    And holy is his Name.
And his mercy is on them that fear him
    Throughout all generations.
He hath shewéd strength with his arm;
He hath scattered the proud in the imagination of their hearts.
He hath put down the mighty from their seat,
    And hath exalted the humble and meek.
He hath filléd the hungry with good things,
    And the rich he hath sent empty away.
He remembering his mercy hath holpen his servant Israel,
    As he promised to out forefathers,
    Abraham and his seed for ever.
Glory be to the Father and to the Son,
    And to the Holy Ghost.
As it was in the beginning, is now, and ever shall be:
    World without end. Amen.

O COME, O COME, EMMANUEL
Veni, Veni, Emmanuel
Latin Antiphons, 12th century
Translated by John Mason Neale, 1818–1866
This haunting carol is the epitome of an Advent hymn. John Mason Neale, the gifted translator and hymn writer, based the 1851 text for *O Come, O Come, Emmanuel* on the "O" antiphons that are a series of chants sung at vespers on the evenings leading up to Christmas. They begin with such words as "O Wisdom," "O Adonai," O Root of Jesse," "O Key of David," "O Dayspring," and of course "O Emmanuel." The tune to this carol was probably written in the 13th century. The text of this hymn is filled with many Biblical allusions and a firm understanding of Covenantal theology. Some of the more important concepts are here identified. The word "Emmanuel" means "God with us" and directly refers to Isaiah 7:14 as well as Matthew 1:23. The word "Israel" refers to all Christians, and the reference to the Babylonian exile is a metaphor for the fallen state of man who is banned from paradise. The "Branch of Jesse" in verse two is part of the messianic prophecy found in Isaiah 11:1. This verse also refers to the crushing of Satan's power through the harrowing of hell by Christ just before his resurrection. The image of the morning star or daystar is invoked in verse three with a clear connection to Malachi 4:2. The messianic prophecy of Isaiah 22:22 is mentioned in verse four with the reference to the Key of David. The word "Adonai" in verse five means "Lord" and was one of the substituted titles for the Name of God (which devout Jews considered unutterable). The rest of the verse refers to the giving of the Ten Commandments that were fulfilled in the person of Christ.

O come, O come, Emmanuel,
And ransom captive Israel,
That mourns in lonely exile here,
Until the Son of God appear.

Rejoice! Rejoice! Emmanuel
Shall come to thee, O Israel.

O come, thou Branch of Jesse! Draw
The quarry from the lion's claw;
From the dread caverns of the grave,
From nether hell, thy people save.

O come, O come, thou Dayspring bright!
Pour on our souls thy healing light;
Dispel the long night's lingering gloom,
And pierce the shadows of the tomb.

O come, thou Key of David, come
And open wide our heavenly home;
Safeguard the way that leads on high,
And close the path to misery.

O come, O come, Adonai,
Who in thy glorious majesty
From Sinai's mountain, clothed in awe,
Gavest thy folk the elder law.

SAVIOUR OF THE NATIONS, COME
Veni, Redemptor gentium
Ambrose of Milan, 340–397
Translated from the Latin by Martin Luther, 1483-1546
Translated from the German by William M. Reynolds, 1860
Ambrose was the great bishop of Milan who was instrumental in the conversion of St. Augustine. In fact, there is evidence in one of Augustine's writings that substantiates Ambrose's authorship of this hymn. Ambrose is credited with writing several hymns and is sometimes referred to as the Father of Hymnody. This hymn was traditionally sung at the first vespers service of the Nativity on Christmas Eve. Church Reformer, Martin Luther was instrumental in popularizing this hymn in Germany through his 1524 translation of the Latin. The following version is a translation from Luther's German text by William M. Reynolds. Several versions of this hymn exist, including a fine translation by John Mason Neale *(Come, Thou Redeemer of the Earth)*.

Saviour of the nations, come,
　　Virgin's Son, make here thy home!
Marvel now, O heaven and earth,
　　That the Lord chose such a birth.

Not of flesh and blood the Son,
　　Offspring of the Holy One;
Born of Mary ever blest
　　God in flesh is manifest.

Wondrous birth! O wondrous Child
　　Of the virgin undefiled!
Though by all the world disowned,
　　Still to be in heaven enthroned.

From the Father forth he came
　　And returneth to the same,
Captive leading death and hell,
　　High the song of triumph swell!

Thou, the Father's only Son,
　　Hast o'er sin the victory won.
Boundless shall thy kingdom be;
　　When shall we its glories see?

Praise to God the Father sing,
　　Praise to God the Son, our King,
Praise to God the Spirit be
　　Ever and eternally.

O HOW SHALL I RECEIVE THEE
Paul Gerhardt, 1607–1676
Translated by Arthur Tozer Russell, 1851
Paul Gerhardt is recognized as one of the great German hymn writers.
Gerhardt was a Lutheran minister during a period of civil unrest and
despite personal tragedies persisted in his calling and wrote over 130
hymns. His best known Christmas hymn is *All My Heart This Night Rejoice;*

however, *O How Shall I Receive Thee* is a fine example of a true Advent hymn because of its allusion to Christ's ultimate triumphal return. This hymn in the original German has ten stanzas and was published in 1653. It is based on Matthew 21:1-9, the story of Jesus and the Triumphal entry into Jerusalem on the back of a donkey on Palm Sunday. This passage is usually the gospel reading for the first Sunday in Advent.

O how shall I receive thee,
    How greet thee, Lord, aright?
All nations long to see thee,
    My Hope, my heart's delight!
O kindle, Lord most holy,
    Thy lamp within my breast,
To do in spirit lowly
    All that may please thee best.

Thy Zion palms is strewing,
    And branches fresh and fair;
My heart, its powers renewing,
    An anthem shall prepare.
My soul puts off her sadness
    Thy glories to proclaim;
With all her strength and gladness
    She fain would serve thy Name.

Love caused thine incarnation,
    Love brought thee down to me;
Thy thirst for my salvation

Procured my liberty.
O love beyond all telling
   That led thee to embrace,
In love all love excelling,
   Our lost and fallen race.

Rejoice then, ye sad-hearted,
   Who sit in deepest gloom,
Who mourn o're joys departed
   And tremble at your doom,
He who alone can cheer you
   Is standing at the door;
He brings his pity near you,
   And bids you weep no more.

OF THE FATHER'S LOVE BEGOTTEN
Corde natus ex Parentis
Aurelius Clemens Prudentius, 348–413
Translated by John Mason Neale, 1818–1866
Rarely in one carol does an author encompass the entirety of the
Redemption story from creation, the prophets, the nativity, and the eternal
glory of the Triune God, but Spanish poet Prudentius skillfully weaves the
redemptive narrative throughout the verses of this fine poem.
Consequently, these lyrics are also dense with the theology of the
Sovereignty of God and his perfect oversight of history. Prudentius was a
well-educated lawyer, judge, and chief of Emperor Honorius' imperial
bodyguard. He exchanged all of his worldly success for spiritual contempla-

tion when he entered a monastery late in life. It took someone like the English clergyman John Mason Neale, a Greek and Latin scholar, to translate and adequately convey the power and poetry of the original text.

Of the Father's love begotten.
    Ere the worlds began to be,
He is Alpha and Omega,
    He the Source, the Ending he.
Of the things that are, that have been,
    And that future years shall see Evermore and evermore.

O that birth forever blessèd!
    When the Virgin full of grace,
By the Holy Ghost conceiving,
    Bore the Savior of our race,
And the babe, the world's Redeemer,
    First revealed his sacred face Evermore and evermore.

He assumed this mortal body,
    Frail and feeble, doomed to die,
That the race from dust created
    Might not perish utterly,
Which the dreadful Law had sentenced
    In the depths of hell to lie Evermore and evermore.

This is he whom once the sibyls
    With united voice foretold,
Whom the Scriptures of the prophets

Promised in their faithful word.
Let the world unite to praise him,
   Long desired, foreseen of old Evermore and evermore.

O ye heights of heaven adore him!
   Angel hosts, his praises sing!
All dominions bow before him,
   And extol your God and King!
Let no tongue on earth be silent,
   Every voice in concert ring Evermore and evermore.

Christ, to Thee, with God the Father,
   And, O Holy Ghost to Thee,
Hymn, and chant, and high thanksgiving,
   And unwearied praises be,
Honour, glory, and dominion,
   And eternal victory, Evermore and evermore.

LO! HE COMES WITH CLOUDS DESCENDING
Verses 1, 2 — Charles Wesley, 1707–1788
Verses 3, 4 — John Cennick, 1718–1755
Verse 5 — Wesley and Cennick
Charles Wesley, the prolific Methodist reformer and hymn writer, discovered John Cennick's hymn in the fifth edition of Cennick's *Collection of Sacred Hymns* (1758). Wesley was drawn to the theme of the Second

Coming of Christ, which is a traditional subject of meditation during the penitential season of Advent, and he wrote additional lyrics to the already vivid and almost epic language. Unfortunately, this fine hymn is often neglected—especially during the Advent season.

Lo! he comes with clouds descending, once for favored sinners slain;
    Thousand thousand saints attending swell the triumph of his train.
Alleluia! Alleluia! God appears on earth to reign.

Every eye shall now behold him, robed in dreadful majesty;
    Those who set at naught and sold him, pierced, and nailed him
    to the tree,
Deeply wailing, deeply wailing, shall the true Messiah see.

Every island, sea, and mountain, heaven and earth, shall flee away;
    All who hate him must, confounded, hear the trump proclaim the day:
Come to judgment! Come to judgment! Come to judgment, come away!

Now Redemption, long expected, see in solemn pomp appear!
    All his saints, by man rejected, now shall meet him in the air.
Alleluia! Alleluia! See the day of God appear!

Yea, Amen! let all adore Thee, High on Thine eternal throne;
    Saviour, take the power and glory, Claim the kingdom for Thine own:
O come quickly, O come quickly; Alleluia! come, Lord, come!

O SOLUS ORTUS CARDINE
From Lands That See The Sun Arise
Coelius Sedlius, c. 450
vv. 1, 5, 8 translated by John Mason Neale, 1818–1866
vv. 2–4, 6, 7 translated by J. Ellerton, 1826–1893
This poem by Coelius Sedlius is part of a larger poem on the life of Christ
called *Pæan Alphabetocus de Christo*. In the original Latin, this poem is an
acrostic poem in which the first letters of each stanza are successive letters
of the alphabet. This part of the larger work is letters A through G with an
added doxology. It was standard to conclude a poem or hymn with a doxological stanza that is simply a verse of praise to the triune God—Father,
Son, and Holy Ghost. Verse five contains a reference to Mary's meeting
with her cousin Elizabeth. This is another example of John Mason Neale's
ability as a translator of Latin texts as well as J. Ellerton.

From lands that see the sun arise
    To earth's remotest boundaries
Let every heart awake, and sing
    The Son of Mary, Christ the King.

Behold, the world's Creator wears
    The form and fashion of a slave;
Our very flesh our Maker shares,
    His fallen creature, man, to save.

For this, how wondrously he wrought!
    A maiden, in her lowly place,

Became, in ways beyond all thought,
    The chosen vessel of his grace.

She bowed her to the angel's word
    Declaring what the Father willed;
And suddenly the promised Lord
    That pure and holy temple filled.

That Son, that royal Son she bore,
    Whom Gabriel announced before,
Whom, in his mother's womb concealed,
    The unborn Baptist had revealed.

And, while the angels in the sky
    Sang praise above the silent field,
To shepherds poor the Lord most high,
    The one great Shepherd was revealed.

Eternal praise and glory be,
    O Jesu, virgin-born, to thee,
With Father and with Holy Ghost,
    From men and from the heav'nly host.

Gloria tibi, Domine,
    Qui natus es de Virgine,
Cum Patre et Sancto Spiritu,
    In sempiterna secula. Amen.

BREAK FORTH, O BEAUTEOUS HEAVENLY LIGHT
Brich an, du schones Morgenlicht
Johann Rist, 1607–1667
Johann Rist was a physician and pastor in Wedel, Germany. He wrote near-ly 700 hymns and was honored as poet laureate in 1645 by Emperor Ferdinand III. Despite this, *Break Forth, O Beauteous Heavenly Light* is essentially the only hymn that is remembered from his work. Johann Sebastian Bach (1685–1750) preserved this poem by utilizing these lyrics and harmonizing their accompanying melody in his famous 1734 Christmas Oratorio.

Break forth, O beauteous heavenly light,
    And usher in the morning;
Ye shepherds, shrink not with affright,
    But hear the angel's warning.
This Child, now born in infancy,
    Our confidence and joy shall be,
The power of Satan breaking,
    Our peace eternal making.

All blessing, thanks and praise to thee,
    Lord Jesus Christ, be given:
Thou hast our brother deigned to be,
    Our foes in sunder riven.
O grant us through our day of grace
    With constant praise to seek thy face;
Grant us ere long in glory
    With praises to adore thee.

COME, THOU LONG-EXPECTED JESUS
Charles Wesley, 1707–1788
Writing often on the love of God, Charles Wesley published some four thousand hymns and left two thousand more in manuscript form. This advent carol is one of his first hymns, published in 1744 in a small book called *Hymns for the Nativity of Our Lord.* Based on Haggai 2:7 ("And I will shake all nations, and the Desire of Nations shall come and I will fill this house with glory," saith the Lord of Hosts.), this hymn portrays the Messianic reign over the hearts of men forever.

Come, Thou long-expected Jesus,
 Born to set Thy people free;
From our fears and sins release us;
 Let us find our rest in Thee.
Israel's Strength and Consolation,
 Hope of all the earth Thou art;
Dear Desire of every nation,
 Joy of every longing heart.

Born Thy people to deliver,
 Born a child, and yet a King,
Born to reign in us forever,
 Now Thy gracious Kingdom bring.
By Thine own eternal Spirit
 Rule in our hearts alone;
By Thine all-sufficient merit
 Raise us to Thy glorious throne.

HARK! AN AWE-FULL VOICE IS SOUNDING
Vox clara ecce intonat
5th–10th century
Translated by Edward Caswall, 1814–1878
Edward Caswall translated almost two hundred hymns from Latin. This particular hymn is of unknown origin and may date anywhere from the fifth to the tenth century. The text is well suited to Advent, and was used for Lauds (sunrise) services during the first week of Advent and then used daily until Christmas Eve. Caswall was an Anglican priest who converted to Catholicism. He spent the last part of his life ministering to the sick and poor in and around Birmingham, England.

Hark! An awful voice is sounding;
 "Christ is nigh," it seems to say;
"Cast away the dreams of darkness,
 O ye children of the day!"

Wakened by the solemn warning,
 Let the earth-bound soul arise;
Christ, her Sun, all ill dispelling,
 Shines upon the morning skies.

Lo! The Lamb, so long expected,
 Comes with pardon down from heaven,
Let us haste, with tears of sorrow,
 One and all to be forgiven;

That, when next He comes with glory,
    And the world is wrapped in fear,
With His mercy He may shield us,
    And with words of love draw near.

Honor, glory, might, and blessing
    To the Father and the Son,
With the Everlasting Spirit
    While eternal ages run. Amen.

THE LORD AT FIRST DID ADAM MAKE
English Traditional Carol
Based on Genesis 3, this carol relates the Fall of man and the doctrine of
original sin that is "wrapt" around Adam and his offspring; however, the
final stanza introduces the hope of salvation through the substitutionary
sacrifice of God's own Son. An understanding of the doctrines of sin and
grace is part of the penitential nature of the Advent season.

The Lord at first did Adam make
    Out of the dust and clay,
And in his nostrils breathed life
    E'en as the scriptures say.
And then in Eden's paradise
    He placéd him to dwell,
That he within it should remain,
    To dress and keep it well:

Now let good Christians all begin
An holy life to live,
And to rejoice and merry be,
For this is Christmas Eve.

And thus within the garden he
    Was set therein to stay;
And in commandment unto him
    These words the Lord did say:
'The fruit which in the garden grows
    To thee shall be for meat,
Except the tree in the midst thereof,
    Of which thou shalt not eat:'

For in the day thou shalt it touch
    Or dost to it come nigh,
If so thou do but eat thereof
    Then thou shalt surely die.
But Adam he did take no heed
    Unto that only thing,
But did transgress God's holy law,
    And so was wrapt in sin:

Now mark the goodness of the Lord,
    Which he for mankind bore;
His mercy soon he did extend,
    Lost man for to restore;
And then, for to redeem our souls

From death and hellish thrall,
He said his own dear Son should be
   The Saviour of us all.

BEHOLD, THE BRIDEGROOM DRAWETH NIGH
Translated from the Greek by Rev. R. M. Moorsom, 1901
At midnight there was a cry made, Behold the bridegroom cometh; go ye out to meet him. Matthew 25:6
The parable of the Wise and Foolish Virgins provides the basis for this advent carol from the Greek Orthodox Church. The five virgins who were prepared and waiting for the bridegroom are a reminder of the penitential nature of advent as a time of preparation for the return of Christ. As surely as he was incarnate in the form of a baby at Christmas, he will return as the victorious Savior at the great doxological dénouement of Judgment Day.

"Behold the Bridegroom draweth nigh;"
   Hear ye the oft-repeated cry?
Go forth into the midnight dim;
   For blessed are they whom He shall find
With ready heart and watchful mind;
   Go forth, my soul, to Him.

"Behold the Bridegroom cometh by,"
   The call is echo'd from the sky:
Go forth, ye servants, watch and wait;
   The slothful cannot join His train;
No careless one may entrance gain;
   Awake, my soul, 'tis late.

The wise will plead with one accord,
   "O Holy, Holy, Holy Lord,
On us Thy quickening grace bestow,
   That none may reach to door too late,
When Thou shalt enter at the gate
   And to Thy kingdom go."

"Behold the Bridegroom draweth near,"
   The warning falls on every ear:
That night of dread shall come to all:
   Behold, my soul, thy lame so dim,
Rise, rise the smoking flax to trim;
   Soon shalt thou hear His call.

THIS IS THE TRUTH SENT FROM ABOVE
English Traditional
Part of the preparation of Advent is the understanding and realization of
Man's sinfulness. This traditional English carol is part of a genre of songs
and poems that are a reminder of how sin came into the world (Genesis 3),
but also how the promise of a Savior was made at this same time. Even
while cursing Adam and Eve for their disobedience, God also revealed his
grace in the form of a promise that the head of the serpent would be
crushed by the Blest Redeemer, his own Son.

This is the truth sent from above,
   The truth of God, the God of love;

Therefore don't turn me from the door,
    But hearken all, both rich and poor.

The first thing that I will relate,
    That God at first did man create;
The next thing which to you I tell
    Woman was made with him to dwell.

Then after that 'twas God's own choice
    To place them both in paradise,
There to remain from evil free
    Except they ate of such a tree.

But they did eat, which was a sin,
    And thus their ruin did begin–
Ruined themselves, both you and me,
    And all of our posterity.

Thus we were heirs to endless woes
    Till God the Lord did interpose;
And so a promise soon did run:
    That he'd redeem us by his Son.

But Our blest Redeemer thus behaved,
    And told us how we must be saved;
"And he that does believe on me,
    From all his sins I'll set him free."

God grant to all within this place
  True-saving faith, that special grace
Which to his people doth belong:
  And thus I close my Christmas song.

WAKE, AWAKE, FOR NIGHT IS FLYING
Wachet auf! Ruft uns die Stimme
Philipp Nicolai, 1556–1608
Translated by Catherine Winkworth, 1829–1878
Philipp Nicolai composed the words and music for this "King of Chorales" in 1599, the same year that he wrote his other most famous work, *How Brightly Beams the Morning Star*. What makes this accomplishment even more amazing is the circumstances surrounding their composition. In the 1590's, Nicolai was a Lutheran pastor in Unna, Westphalia, during the time when more than 1300 people died from the bubonic plague in a period of six months. As many as 30 burials occurred each day during the period from July 1597, to January 1598, and Nicolai's home, the Lutheran rectory, overlooked the cemetery. On August 10, 1598, he wrote the preface to his book, *Mirror of Joy*. In it he writes: "There seems to me nothing more sweet, delightful, and agreeable, than the contemplation of the noble, sublime doctrine of Eternal Life, obtained through the Blood of Christ. This I allow to dwell in my heart day and night, and search the Scriptures as to what they revealed on this matter, read also the sweet treatise of the ancient doctor St. Augustine *[De Civitate Dei}*....Then day by day I wrote out of my meditations, found myself, thank God! wonderfully well, comforted in heart, joyful in spirit, truly content; gave to my manuscript the name and title of a Mirror of Joy, and took this, thus composed, to leave behind me (if

God should call me from the world) as the token of my peaceful, joyful, Christian departure, or (if God should spare me in health) to comfort other sufferers." The words are based on Matthew 25:1-13, Revelation 19:6–9 and 21:21, 1 Corinthians 2:9, Ezekiel 3:17, and Isaiah 52:8. Felix Mendelssohn integrated the chorale melody into his St. Paul, and Johann Sebastian Bach (1685–1750) used both words and music for his Cantata No. 140, written for the 27th Sunday after Trinity, November 25, 1731—part of the Church year calendar.

Wake, awake, for night is flying,
The watchmen on the heights are crying,
    Awake, Jerusalem, at last!
Midnight hears the welcome voices
And at the thrilling cry rejoices:
    Come forth, ye virgins, night is past!
The Bridegroom comes, awake,
Your lamps with gladness take;
    Alleluia!
And for his marriage feast prepare,
For ye must go to meet him there.

Zion hears the watchmen singing,
And all her heart with joy is springing,
    She wakes, she rises from her gloom;
For her Lord comes down all-glorious,
The strong in grace, in truth victorious,
    Her star is risen, her Light is come.
Ah come, thou blesséd One,

God's own belovéd Son,
    Alleluia!
We follow till the halls we see
Where thou hast bid us sup with thee.

Now let all the heavens adore thee,
And men and angels sing before thee,
    With harp and cymbal's clearest tone;
Of one pearl each shining portal,
Where we are with the choir immortal
    Of angels round thy dazzling throne;
Nor eye hath seen, nor ear
Hath yet attained to hear
    What there is ours;
But we rejoice, and sing to thee
Our hymn of joy eternally.

THE KING SHALL COME WHEN MORNING DAWNS
Translated from the Greek by John Brownlie, 1859–1925
This hymn from the Eastern Orthodox tradition is a typical Advent carol
with its anticipation of the coming King. This is a theme that is echoed not
only in the Incarnation but also in the Triumphal Entry of Christ into
Jerusalem before his crucifixion and his Second Coming.

The King shall come when morning dawns
    And light triumphant breaks;
When beauty gilds the eastern hills
    And life to joy awakes.

Not as of old, a little child,
  To bear, and fight, and die;
But crowned with glory like the sun
  That lights the morning sky.

The King shall come when morning dawns,
  And earth's dark night is past;
O haste the rising of that morn,
  The day that aye shall last;

And let the endless bliss begin,
  By weary saints foretold,
When right shall triumph over wrong,
  And truth shall be extolled.

The King shall come when morning dawns,
  And light and beauty brings:
Hail, Christ the Lord! Thy people pray,
  Come quickly, King of kings. Amen.

COMFORT, COMFORT YE
Troestet, troestet meine Lieben
Johannes Olearius, 1611–1684
Translated by Catherine Winkworth, 1829–1878
This hymn was originally written for St. John the Baptist's Day, and as
such, it is quite appropriate for Advent as it speaks of the voice crying out
in the desert. It is based on Isaiah 40:1-5, one of the main texts read in con-
junction with Advent and the coming of the Messiah.

Comfort, comfort ye, my people,
　　Speak ye peace, thus saith our God;
Comfort those who sit in darkness,
　　Bowed beneath their sorrow's load;
Of the peace that waits for them
　　Speak ye to Jerusalem;
Tell her that her sins I cover,
　　And her warfare now is over.

Yea, her sins our God will pardon,
　　Blotting out each dark misdeed;
All that well deserved his anger
　　He will no more see or heed.
She hath suffered many a day,
　　Now her griefs have passed away,
God will change her pining sadness
　　Into ever-springing gladness.

For the herald's voice is crying
　　In the desert far and near,
Bidding all men to repentance,
　　Since the kingdom now is here.
O, that warning cry obey!
　　Now prepare for God a way;
Let the valleys rise to meet him,
　　And the hills bow down to greet him.

Make ye straight what long was crooked,
    Make the rougher places plain
Let your hearts be true and humble,
    As befits his holy reign;
For the glory of the Lord
    Now o'er earth is shed abroad,
And all flesh shall see the token
    That his word is never broken.

HARK THE GLAD SOUND!
Philip Doddridge, 1702–1751
The English Puritan Philip Doddridge was the youngest of twenty children. His parents died when he was a boy, and he was raised by friends of
the family. Because he could not accept the tenets of the Anglican church,
he refused an offer to attend Cambridge and went to a non-conforming
seminary instead. At the age of twenty-seven, Doddridge began to pastor
the Castle Hill congregational chapel in Northampton, England where he
remained for twenty-two years. He spent much of his time in Northampton
in training other young men for the ministry in independent churches. He
taught about two hundred men Hebrew, Greek, math, philosophy, Bible,
and theology. He wrote several books on theology and over four hundred
hymns. Many of his hymns were written as summaries of his sermons so
that the congregation was able to express their response to the truths
taught. Always plagued by ill health, Doddridge contracted tuberculosis and
died in Lisbon, Portugal, while seeking a respite from the disease.

Hark the glad sound! The Saviour comes,
  The Saviour promised long:
Let every heart prepare a throne,
  And every voice a song.

He comes, the prisoners to release
  In Satan's bondage held;
The gates of brass before Him burst,
  The iron fetters yield.

He comes, the broken heart to bind,
  The bleeding soul to cure,
And with the treasures of His grace
  To bless the humble poor.

Our glad hosannas, Prince of peace,
  Thy welcome shall proclaim,
And heaven's eternal arches ring
  With Thy beloved Name.

Advent Ballads and Verse

The Angel Gabriel
Anonymous
The story of the Annunciation has for centuries been a favorite for ballads, carols, paintings, and icons. The occasion of the angel Gabriel announcing to the Virgin Mary the birth of the Messiah is high drama indeed! As a typical ballad that tells a story, *The Angel Gabriel* relates the narrative of the angel's visit as outlined in the Gospel of Luke 1:26-38.

I
The Angel Gabriel from God
    Was sent to Galilee,
Unto a Virgin fair and free,
    Whose name was called Mary:
And when the Angel thither came,
    He fell down on his knee,
And looking up in the virgin's face,
    He said, 'All hail, Mary!'
Then, sing we all, both great and small,
    Noël, Noël, Noël;
We may rejoice to hear the voice
    Of the Angel Gabriel.

II
Mary anon looked him upon,
    And said, 'Sir, what are ye?
I marvel much at these tidings

Which thou hast brought to me.
Married I am unto an old man,
 As the lot fell unto me;
Therefore, I pray, depart away,
 For I stand in doubt of thee.'
Then, sing, &c.

III

'Mary,' he said, 'be not afraid,
 But do believe in me:
The power of the Holy Ghost
 Shall overshadow thee,
Thou shalt conceive without any grief,
 As the Lord told unto me;
God's own dear Son from Heaven shall come,
 And shall be born of thee.'
Then, sing, &c.

IV

This came to pass as God's will was,
 Even as the Angel told.
About midnight an Angel bright
 Came to the Shepherds' fold,
And told them then both where and when
 Born was the child, our Lord
And all along this was their song,
 'All glory be given to God.'
Then, sing, &c.

V

Good people all, both great and small,
　　The which do hear my voice,
With one accord let's praise the Lord,
　　And in our hearts rejoice;
Like sister and brother, let's love one another
　　Whilst we our lives do spend,
Whilst we have space let's pray for grace,
　　And so let my Carol end.
Then, sing, &c.

ADAM LAY Y-BOUNDEN
Anonymous, c. 1450
This beautiful ballad comes from an anonymous English manuscript from
the fifteenth century. It tells of the bonds of original sin that enslaved all
people until the coming of the Savior. It is part of a traditional body of literature from the Medieval era that considers the entrance of sin into the
world as a blessed opportunity for God to show forth his grace.

Adam lay y-bounden
　　Bounden in a bond;
Four thousand winter
　　Thought he not too long;
And all was for an apple
　　An apple that he took,
As clerkes finden written
　　In theire book.

Ne had the apple taken been,
    The apple taken been,
Ne hadde never our Lady
    A been heaven's queen.
Blessed be the time
    That apple taken was!
Therefore we may singen
    'Deo Gratias!'

Prayers for Advent

Prayer for the First Sunday of Advent
Book of Common Prayer, 1789
Almighty God, give us grace
    that we may cast away the works of darkness,
    and put upon us the armor of light,
now in the time of this mortal life
    in which thy Son Jesus Christ came to visit us in great humility;
that in the last day,
    when he shall come again in his glorious majesty
    to judge both the quick and the dead,
we may rise to the life immortal;
    through him who liveth and reigneth with thee
    and the Holy Ghost,
        one God, now and for ever. *Amen.*

Prayer for the Second Sunday of Advent
Book of Common Prayer, 1789
Merciful God,
    who didst send thy messengers the prophets
        to preach repentance
        and prepare the way for our salvation:
Give us grace to heed their warnings and forsake our sins,
that we may greet with joy the coming of Jesus Christ our Redeemer;
who liveth and reigneth with thee
    and the Holy Spirit,
    one God, now and for ever. *Amen.*

PRAYER FOR THE THIRD SUNDAY OF ADVENT
Book of Common Prayer, 1789
Stir up thy power, O Lord,
   and with great might come among us;
and, because we are sorely hindered by our sins,
   let thy bountiful grace and mercy speedily help and deliver us;
through Jesus Christ our Lord,
   to whom, with thee and the Holy Ghost,
   be honor and glory,
   world without end. Amen.

PRAYER FOR THE FOURTH SUNDAY OF ADVENT
Book of Common Prayer, 1789
We beseech thee, Almighty God,
   to purify our consciences by thy daily visitation,
that when thy Son our Lord cometh
   he may find in us a mansion prepared for himself;
through the same Jesus Christ our Lord,
   who liveth and reigneth with thee,
   in the unity of the Holy Spirit,
one God, now and for ever. *Amen.*

Daily Readings for Advent

First Sunday in Advent
Genesis 3:1-15 — The Fall of Man and the first promise of the Messiah is revealed.

Monday
Genesis 22:15-18 — God promises to faithful Abraham that in his seed all nations of the earth shall be blessed.

Tuesday
Isaiah 7:14 & 9:2-7 — Christ's birth and kingdom are foretold by the prophet Isaiah.

Wednesday
Isaiah 11:1-9 — A rod shall come forth from the stem of Jesse.

Thursday
Micah 5:2-4 — The glory of little Bethlehem is foretold by the prophet Micah.

Friday
Malachi 4:1-3 — The Sun of Righteousness, the Daystar, shall arise.

Saturday
Numbers 24:15-19; 2 Peter 1:19; Revelation 22:16 — The verity of the prophecies are confirmed.

SECOND SUNDAY IN ADVENT
Exodus 20:1-17 — The Law of God that we in our own strength cannot keep.

MONDAY
Joel 2: 12,13 — The Lord desires a repentant heart.

TUESDAY
Isaiah 40:1-11 — Comfort ye my people.

WEDNESDAY
Romans 3:21-28 — Righteousness by the Law of Faith through Christ.

THURSDAY
Romans 8:1-4 — The fulfillment of the Law through Christ.

FRIDAY
Isaiah 60:1-4 — Arise, shine! for your light has come.

SATURDAY
Hebrews 10:1-10 — Christ came to fulfill the need for an all-sufficient sacrifice for sins.

THIRD SUNDAY IN ADVENT
Luke 1:5-17 — The birth of John the Baptist is foretold to Zacharias.

MONDAY
Luke 1:13-25 — Zacharias is struck dumb until the fulfillment of Gabriel's prophecy.

TUESDAY
Luke 1:26-38 — The angel Gabriel's annunciation to the Virgin Mary of the Incarnation.

WEDNESDAY
Matthew 1:18-25 — The angel of the Lord comes to Joseph in a dream.

THURSDAY
Luke 1:39-56 — Mary visits Elizabeth, the mother of John the Baptist.

FRIDAY
Luke 1:57-66 — The birth of John the Baptist.

SATURDAY
Luke 1: 67-80 — Zacharias speaks a prophecy over the infant John.

FOURTH SUNDAY IN ADVENT
Luke 2:1-7 — St. Luke tells of the birth of Jesus.

MONDAY
Micah 4:1-7 — All nations shall find peace from the God of Jacob.

TUESDAY
Luke 2:8-14 — The angels proclaim the birth of Christ to the shepherds.

WEDNESDAY
Psalm 98 — The Lord has made known his salvation.

THURSDAY
Luke 2:15-20 — The shepherds go to the manger.

FRIDAY
Philippians 2:5-11 — The humility of Christ.

SATURDAY
Titus 2:11-3:7 — The grace of God that brings salvation has appeared to all men.

S<small>T.</small> B<small>ONIFACE AND THE</small> L<small>ITTLE</small> P<small>ASCHA</small>

Let us standfast in what is right and prepare our souls for trial. Let us be neither dogs that do not bark nor silent onlookers nor paid servants who run away before the wolf.
B<small>ONIFACE OF</small> C<small>REDITON</small> (680–755)

Boniface of Crediton spent the first forty years of his life in quiet service to the church near his home in Exeter. He discipled young converts, cared for the sick, and administered relief for the poor. He was a competent scholar as well, expounding Bible doctrine for a small theological center and compiling the first Latin grammar written in England. But in 718, Boniface left the comfort and security of this life to become a missionary to the savage Teutonic tribes of Germany. For thirty years he not only proclaimed to them the Gospel of Light, he portrayed to them the Gospel of Life. Stories of his courageous intervention on behalf of the innocent abound. He was constantly jeopardizing his own life for the sake of the young, the vulnerable, the weak, the helpless, the aged, the sick, and the poor—often imposing his body between the victims and their oppressors. Indeed, it was during one of his famed rescues that his name was forever linked to the celebration of Advent during Yuletide.

Wherever he went among the fierce Norsemen who had settled along the Danish and German coast, he was forced to face the awful specter of their brutal pagan practices—that included human mutilations and vestal sacrifices. When he arrived in the region of Hesse, Boniface decided to strike at the root of such superstitions. He publicly announced that he would destroy their gods. He then marched toward their great sacred grove. The awestruck crowd at Geismar followed along and then watched as he cut down the sacred Oak of Thor, an ancient object of pagan worship standing atop the summit of Mount Gudenberg near Fritzlar. The pagans, who had expected immediate judgment against such sacrilege, were forced to acknowledge that their gods were powerless to protect their own sanctuaries. Together, they professed faith in Christ.

A young boy from a neighboring village, hearing of such boldness, rushed into the missionary camp of Boniface three evenings later. It was just about twilight on the first Sunday in Advent. He breathlessly told of a sacrifice that was to be offered that very evening—his sister was to serve as the vestal virgin.

Hurrying through the snowy woods and across the rough terrain, Boniface and the boy arrived at the dense sacred grove just in time to see the Druid priest raise his knife into the darkened air. But as the blade plunged downward Boniface hurtled toward the horrid scene. He had nothing in his hands save a small wooden cross. Lunging forward, he reached the girl just in time to see the blade of the knife pierce the cross—thus, saving her life.

The priest toppled back. The huddle of worshipers were astonished. There was a brief moment of complete silence. Boniface seized upon it. He proclaimed the Gospel to them then and there, declaring that the ultimate sacrifice had already been made by Christ on the cross at Golgotha—there was no need for others.

Captivated by the bizarre scene before them, the small crowd listened intently to his words. After explaining to them the once and for all provision of the Gospel, he turned toward the sacred grove. With the sacrificial knife in hand, he began hacking off low hanging branches. Passing them

around the circle, he told each family to take to the small fir boughs home as a reminder of the completeness of Christ's work on the tree of Calvary. They were to adorn their hearths with the tokens of His grace. They might even chop great logs from the grove as fuel for their home fires, he suggested—not so much to herald the destruction of their pagan ways but rather to memorialize the provision of Christ's coming. Upon these things they were contemplate over the course of the next four weeks, until the great celebration of Christmas.

Such exploits inspired a number of Advent traditions. The Advent wreath—a fir garland set with five candles, one for each Sunday in Advent and one for Christmas Day—was quickly established as a means of reenacting the Gospel lesson of Boniface. In addition, the Christmas tree, decorated with candles and tinsel, strings of lights and garlands under the eaves and across the mantles, and the Yule log burning in the fireplace were favorite reminders of the season's essential message.

In time, Boniface established a number of thriving parishes. He eventually became a mentor and support to the Carolingians, and he reformed the Frankish church, which Charles Martel had plundered. Ultimately, he discipled Pipin the Short, the father of Charlemagne the Great.

Then, when he was over 70, Boniface resigned his pastoral responsibilities, in order to spend his last years working among the fierce Frieslanders. With a small company, he successfully reached large numbers in the previously unevangelized area in the northeastern Germanies. On Whitsun Eve Boniface and Eoban were preparing for the baptism of some of the new converts at Dokkum, along the frontier of the Netherlands. Boniface had been quietly reading in his tent while awaiting the arrival of his new converts, when a hostile band of pagan warriors descended on the camp. He would not allow his companions to defend him. As he was exhorting them to trust in God and to welcome the prospect of dying for the faith, they were attacked—Boniface was one of the first to fall.

Though his voice was stilled that day, his testimony only grew louder, surer, and bolder. And thus, to this day, his message lives on—in the traditions of Advent.

Advent Traditions

Stirring Day

Stirring Day or Stir-Up Sunday, as it is sometimes called is the first Sunday before Advent—usually falling on the Sunday after our American Thanksgiving. A holiday borrowed from the Victorians, it provides a wonderful way to make the transition into the Advent season. On this day mothers and grandmothers gather their whole family into the kitchen, assign various chopping, stirring, measuring, and clean-up tasks and bake the Christmas Plum Pudding together. Then, pudding baked and ageing nicely in a cool, dark spot, they relax with the feeling of satisfaction that although the busy Yuletide season is soon to be upon them, at least some of the preparation for Christmas Dinner was completed. The preparation had begun.

Advent Wreath

Advent begins four Sundays prior to Christmas. For centuries, Christian families have celebrated this season of preparation with the lighting of one candle in a small table-top evergreen wreath each Sunday, accompanied by an appropriate Scripture reading and prayer. The candles vary in color from culture to culture, but generally the first three candles are red or purple and the last one is white or golden. For families that find themselves each year vowing that their celebration of the season will focus more on the real meaning of Christmas and less on the brouhaha, this is the place to begin to set the tone for the holidays.

MARTINMAS
Martin of Umbria (c. 655) was a bishop of Rome who was martyred during the great Monothelite controversy of the seventh century. His perseverance in the face of political persecution, personal humiliation, torture, starvation, and eventually, death, made him a model of faith during the early medieval period. During his final imprisonment, he diligently kept the fasts of the Little Pascha, as Advent was then called, though he was already dying of hunger. Traditionally, Christians have recalled his faithfulness on November 11 by enjoying the last great feast of the season—in England a sumptuous dinner of beef is consumed while in Germany a grand banquet featuring roast goose is served. The new wine is uncasked. Good children receive gifts of fruit and nuts—while naughty children receive little more than sticks, stones, and ashes.

ST. CLEMENT'S DAY
Serving as the bishop of Rome after Peter, Linus, and Cletus at the end of the first century, Clement (c. 100) was one of the greatest stalwarts of the early church. His letters, sermons, and commentaries remain one of the best testimonies of the dynamism of the fledgling Christian witness. A constant encouragement to others, he was responsible for the establishment of at least seventy-five churches. His martyrdom apparently occurred on November 23 and as a result, believers have long remembered him on that day. Celebrated as the first day of winter, it has been marked by community or guild suppers—where co-workers gather to sing, to roast apples, and to offer mutual encouragement in the faith.

St. Catherine's Day

Born into the imperial nobility, Catherine of Alexandria (c. 352) eschewed her privileges, rejected the hand of the emperor in marriage, and ultimately suffered martyrdom for her faith. Her feast day, traditionally celebrated on November 25 with the performance of morality plays followed by a torchlight parade and the singing of hymns—perhaps one of the origins of the tradition of caroling from house to house.

St. Andrew's Day

Numbered among the Apostles, the brother of Simon Peter eventually became the revered patron of both Greece and Scotland where his feast day, November 30, remains a kind of national holiday. Andrew (c. 10–60) may well have been, as tradition asserts, the founder of the church at the site of Constantinople, but he was most assuredly the great reconciler, as Scripture asserts. As a result, his memory is celebrated by a day of forgiveness. Services of reconciliation are often followed by a great feast of roasted or smoked beef, the telling of heroic tales, the reciting epic poetry, and the singing of great ballads.

Klopfelnachte

Literally "Knocking Night," each Thursday in Advent is celebrated throughout German communities by youngsters walking from house to house, beckoning upon the door stoops, singing carols, and offering gifts of fruit and candies. A reversal of the "Trick or Treat" ritual, the Klopfelnachte tradition is a joyous and selfless expression of commitment in a covenantal community.

ST. NICHOLAS DAY

Celebrated on December 6, this day recalls the selfless service of Nicholas of Myra (c. 288–354). The fourth century pastor ultimately inspired the tradition of Santa Claus. In reality, he was a paradigm of graciousness, generosity, and Christian charity. His great love and concern for children drew him into a crusade that ultimately resulted in protective statutes that remained law for more than a thousand years. His feast day is celebrated around the world. In the Netherlands, cookies and gingerbread treats were often placed in the shoes or laid out stockings of sleeping children—which may well have been the origin of Christmas gift and hearthside stockings.

SANTA LUCIA'S DAY

A beautiful and wealthy Sicilian who was martyred during the persecutions of Diocletian, Lucia of Syracuse (c. 304) was known as the patron of light. For her, Advent was always a celebration of the approach of Light and Life. Interestingly, her feast day, held on December 13, is one of the shortest and darkest days of the year. Thus, a great festival of lights is traditionally held in her memory—particularly in Scandinavian cultures. Candles are set into evergreens. Garlands are spread, full of twinkling lights. Torchlight parades are held. And fireworks brighten the evening sky.

ST. THOMAS'S DAY

Though he was doubter at first, the Apostle Thomas (c. 10–60) came to believe that Christ was not only risen from the dead, but proclaimed him "My Lord and my God." His anticipation of the full revelation of the Kingdom is celebrated on December 21. Traditionally this has been a day for well-wishing—friends, neighbors, and loved ones going out of their way to remember other and to bless one another. Though Christmas cards are a

Victorian innovation, they were conceived as a kind of St. Thomas' Day gesture of kindness, encouragement, and graciousness.

YULE LOG
In Serbia and Croatia, the old stories of Boniface and the sacred grove gave rise to the tradition of taking a stout log, boring out its center, filling it with herbs, oil, and wine, and setting it upon the hearth fire—thus filling the home with the sweet fragrance of scented wood smoke. The Yule Log became a vital part of the Advent celebration for Christians throughout central and eastern Europe.

CHRISTMAS TREE
Martin Luther, the great Protestant reformer, condoned the use of the old tradition of Christmas trees. Like the Yule Log, the idea for the Christmas tree was derived over time from the tradition of Boniface and was intended to be a reminder that the idols of this world have been rendered moot while the tree of Calvary has become the very hinge of history. Set in the center of the home and adorned with lights, tinsel, decorative baubles, and topped by a herald angel, the tree was to be a visible representation of the story of the Gospel itself.

MISTLETOE
The little berries of the Mistletoe plant, renowned for their healing powers, became a medieval symbol of God's provision and grace. Even when the vast northern forests were buried in deep snows and the hardwood trees had lost all their foliage, the Mistletoe continued to bloom—to offer its medicine of hope to the afflicted and the needy. Often, families would decorate their doorways with little sprigs of the plant as reminders of provi-

dential love. It became a happy ritual for lovers to kiss beneath the sprigs as a kind of covenantal affirmation of their fealty in the sight of God. A single berry was to be plucked from the sprig for each kiss. Often the bare sprigs were kept as testimony to the couples' vows.

HOLLY AND IVY

Throughout the Celtic lands of Brittany, Cornwall, Wales, Scotland, and Ireland, holly and ivy were symbols of victory won. Holly, representing masculine triumph, and ivy, representing feminine triumph, were often woven together as a sign that men and women need one another. Homes were decorated during Advent with both—often woven together—as a picture of the healthy family under God's gracious providential hand.

LESSONS AND CAROLS

The Service of Lessons and Carols is most closely associated with the King's College Chapel, Cambridge. The service consists of nine Scripture lessons that alternate with carols of a similar theme. The lessons and carols tell of the Fall of Man, the promise of a Savior by the prophets, the annunciation to Mary, the shepherds and angels, and ends with the reading of John chapter one. This Christmas Eve service follows the from laid down by the King's College Dean, Eric Milner-White, in 1918. As he saw it, the strength of the service lay in the scripture readings that outline the need for redemption, the promise of a Savior, and the Nativity itself. Milner-White patterned his service on an Order of Worship drawn up by E. W. Benson, later Archbishop of Canterbury, for use in the wooden shed that then served as his cathedral in Truro for 10 P.M. on Christmas Eve 1880. A.C. Benson recalled: "My father arranged from ancient sources a little service for Christmas Eve—nine carols and nine tiny lessons, which were read by various officers of the Church, beginning with a chorister, and ending, through the different grades, with the Bishop." The suggestion for the service had come from G. H. S. Walpole who later became the Bishop of Edinburgh. The service in Cambridge has been adapted and emulated throughout the world. With the exception of 1930, the BBC has broadcast the concert annually since 1928. This includes the period of the Second World War, when the ancient glass (and also all heat) had been removed from the Chapel and the name of King's College could not be broadcast for security reasons. The combination of prayers, liturgy, carols, Scripture, and congregational worship creates a solemnity that recognizes the historic nature of the Christian faith as well as a celebration of the fulfilled promise of redemption.

TREATS FOR ADVENT

ROAST BEEF

1   8-pound standing 3-rib roast

Place the beef fat-side up in a large shallow roasting pan. Insert a meat thermometer into the thickest part of the beef, being careful not to let the tip of the thermometer touch any fat or bone. Roast the beef undisturbed at 450° in the middle of the oven for 20 minutes. Reduce the heat to 325°, and continue to roast, without basting, for about 90 minutes or until the beef is cooked to taste. (A meat thermometer will register 130° to 140° when the beef is rare, 150° to 160° when medium, and 160° to 170° when it is well done.) If you are not using a thermometer, start timing the roast after you reduce the heat to 325°. Estimate approximately 12 minutes per pound for rare beef, 15 minutes per pound for medium, and 20 minutes per pound for well done.

Transfer the beef to a heated platter, and let it rest for at least 15 minutes for easier carving.

To carve, first remove a thin slice of beef from the large end of the roast so it will stand firmly on this end. Insert a large fork below the top rib and carve slices of beef from the top, separating each slice from the bone. Serve with the pan juices and a horseradish sauce.

Makes 6 to 8 servings.

HASH BROWN QUICHE

12	ounces frozen hash brown potatoes, thawed
⅓	cup butter, melted
3	tablespoons ranch salad dressing
½	teaspoon salt
4	ounces shredded sharp Cheddar cheese
4	ounces shredded Swiss cheese
4	to 6 ounces ham or bacon
½	cup milk
4	eggs
	Dill
	Salt and pepper

In a large bowl mix the potatoes, butter, salad dressing and salt together. Press into a greased 9-inch quiche or baking dish. Bake at 425° for 25 minutes. Fill the crust with cheese and meat. In a small bowl combine the milk and eggs, and add salt, pepper, and dill to taste. Beat well, and pour over the cheese and meat. Bake at 350° for 30 to 40 minutes or until a knife tip inserted near the edge comes out clean.

Makes 6 to 8 servings.

Hot Chocolate Mix

1	medium box powdered milk (8 quart size or 10⅔ cups)
1	small jar powdered French Vanilla coffee creamer
1	pound confectioners' sugar
1	to 1½ pounds chocolate milk mix
¼	teaspoon salt

In a container with a lid combine all of the ingredients. Add ⅓+ cup of mixture to 1 cup hot water.

Cranberry Relish

4	cups cranberries
2	oranges
3	apples
2	cups sugar (or a little less)

In a food processor combine all of the ingredients and process until chopped and well combined.

Sour Cream Gingerbread Cake with Vanilla Sauce

Gingerbread:

2	eggs
½	cup sour cream
½	cup molasses
½	cup firmly packed brown sugar
1½	cup flour
1	teaspoon baking soda
1½	teaspoon ginger
¼	teaspoon salt
½	cup melted butter

Beat the eggs. Add the sour cream, molasses, and brown sugar, and beat well. Add the flour, baking soda, ginger, and salt, and beat well. Beat in the melted butter. Pour in an 8-inch square pan. Bake at 350° for 30 minutes.

Vanilla Sauce:

Yield: 2 cups

2	tablespoons cornstarch
2	cups boiling water
4	tablespoons butter
3	teaspoons vanilla extract
	few grains of salt

In a saucepan mix the sugar and cornstarch to prevent lumps. Add the boiling water gradually, stirring constantly. Boil for 5 minutes until the mixture is clear. Remove from the heat. Add the butter, vanilla, and salt. Serve over warm Gingerbread Cake.

Makes 6 to 8 servings.

Christmas

Christians have celebrated the incarnation and nativity of the Lord Jesus on December 25 since at least the early part of the third century—just a few generations removed the days of the Apostles. By 336, when the Philocalian Calendar—one of the earliest documents of the Patriarchal church—was first utilized, Christmas Day was already a venerable and tenured tradition. Through there is no historical evidence that Christ was actually born on that day—indeed, whatever evidence there is points to altogether different occasions—the conversion of the old Pagan tribes of Europe left a gaping void where the ancient winter cult festivals were once held. It was both culturally convenient and evangelically expedient to exchange the one for the other. And so joy replaced desperation. Celebration replaced propitiation. Christmas feasts replaced new moon sacrifices. Christ replaced Baal, Molech, Apollo, and Thor. Glad tidings of great joy, indeed.

Infinite, and an infant. Eternal, and yet born of a woman. Almighty, and yet hanging on a woman's breast. Supporting a universe, and yet needing to be carried in a mother's arms. King of angels, and yet the reputed son of Joseph. Heir of all things, and yet the carpenter's despised son. Oh, the wonder of Christmas.

Charles Haddon Spurgeon (1834–1892)

The Christ-child lay on Mary's lap
His hair was like a light
O weary, weary were the world
But here is all aright

The Christ-child lay on Mary's breast
His hair was like a star
O stem and cunning are the Kings
But here the true hearts are

The Christ-child lay on Mary's heart
His hair was like a fire
O weary, weary is the world
But here the world's desire

The Christ-child stood at Mary's knee
His hair was like a crown
And all the flowers looked up at Him
And all the stars looked down

G. K. Chesterton (1874–1936)

The love of God which leads to realms above
Is contré-carréd by our notions of a God of Love.
Evidence: Bethlehem's push and Calvary's shove.

Hilaire Belloc (1870–1953)

It was the winter wild
While the heaven-born Child
All meanly wrapt in the rude manger lies;
Nature in awe to Him
Had doff'd her gaudy trim,
With her great Mater so to sympathize:
it was no season then for her
To wanton with the sun, her lusty paramour.

Only with speeches fair
She woos the gentle air
To hide her guilty front with innocent snow;
And on her naked shame,
Pollute with sinful blame,
The saintly veil of maiden white to throw;
Confounded, that her Maker's eyes
Should look so near upon her foul deformities.

But see! The Virgin blest
Hath laid her Babe to rest;
Time is, our tedious song should her have ending:
Heaven's youngest-teemed star
Hath fix'd her polish'd car,
Her sleeping Lord with hand-maid lamp attending:
And all about the courtly stable
Bright-harness'd Angels sit in order serviceable.
John Milton (1608–1674)

Jesus Christ founded His Kingdom on the weakest link of all—a Baby.
Oswald Chambers (1874–1917)

Why, Favourite of Heaven most fair,
Dost thou bring fowls for sacrifice?
Will not the armful thou dost bear,
That lovely Lamb of thine, suffice?
Thomas Bancroft (1544–1610)

Forth they went and glad they were,
Going they did sing;
With mirth and solace they made good cheer
For joy of that new tiding.

Coventry Mystery Play (c. 1200)

Jesus, Lord, we look to thee,
On this day of thine own Nativity;
Show thyself the Prince of Peace;
Bid our jarring conflicts cease.
Let us for each other care,
Each the other's burden bear,
To thy church the pattern give,
Show how true believers live.
Make us one of heart and mind,
Courteous, pitiful, and kind,
Lowly, meek in thought and word,
Altogether like our Lord.

Charles Wesley (1707–1788)

CAROLS AND HYMNS

O CHRIST, THE FATHER'S ONLY SON
Christe, Redemptor Omnium
Sixth-century Translated by John Mason Neale, 1818–1866
This hymn was traditionally sung in the morning at a matins service during the Advent season. John Mason Neale was the gifted clergyman and Greek and Latin scholar. Many of the poetic and literary translations of the great Medieval carols, including *O Come, O Come, Emmanuel* and *Of the Father's Love Begotten*, are due to his skill.

O Christ, the Father's only Son,
    Whose death for all redemption won,
Before the worlds of God most high
    Begotten all ineffably.

The Father's light and splendour thou,
    Their endless hope to thee that bow;
Accept the prayers and praise today
    That through the world thy servants pay.

Salvation's Author, call to mind
    How, taking form of humankind,
Born a virgin undefiled,
    Thou in man's flesh becam'st a child.

Thus testifies the present day,
    Through every year in long array,

That thou, salvation's source alone,
    Proceedest from the Father's throne.

Whence sky, and stars, and sea's abyss,
    And earth, and all that therein is,
Shall still, with laud and carol meet,
    The Author of thine advent greet.

And we who, by thy precious blood
    From sin redeemed, are marked for God,
On this, the day that saw thy birth,
    Sing a new song of ransomed earth.

Eternal praise and glory be,
    O Jesu, virgin-born, to thee,
With Father and with Holy Ghost,
    From men and from the heavenly host.

AS I OUT RODE THIS ENDERES NIGHT
(The Coventry Shepherds' Carol)
16th century
This is one of two songs that are extant from the Coventry Pageant of the
Shearmen and Tailors guilds in the sixteenth century. The pageant was a
didactic tool used by the Church in Coventry, England, to teach the people
about the Bible and theology. These plays were performed on carts drawn
through the streets. Right before the introduction of the shepherds in this
particular play, Mary sends Joseph in search of a midwife because the birth

of Christ is imminent. As three shepherds gather together for food and
shelter, the star is revealed, and the third shepherd exclaims:

> A ha! Now ys cum the tyme that old fathurs [prophets] hath told,
> Thatt in the wynturs nyght soo cold
> A chyld of meydyn borne be he wold
> In whom all profeciys schalbe fullfyld.

The angels sing "'Glorea in excelsis Deo' above in the clowdis." The first
shepherd suggests:

> . . . mow goo we hence
> To worschippe thatt chyld of hy manyffecence,
> And that we ma syng in his prescence
> "Et in tarra pax omynibus. "

The shepherds sing the first verse of "Ase I owt Rodde" followed by dialogue from Joseph, the singing of the angels, and a blessing from Mary.
"There the Scheppardis syngith ageyne and goth forthe of the place."

As I out rode this enderes [the other] night,
   Of thre joli sheppardes I saw a sight,
And all abowte there fold a star shone bright;

They sange 'Terli, terlow!' They sang 'Terli, terlow!'
So mereli the sheppards ther pipes can blow,
ther pipes can blow, so mereli the sheppards,
so mereli the sheppards ther pipes can blow,
ther pipes can blow.
Doune from heaven, from heaven so hie,

Of angels ther came a great companie,
With mirthe and joy and great solemnitye;

They sange 'Terli, terlow!' They sang 'Terli, terlow!'
So mereli the sheppards ther pipes can blow,
ther pipes can blow, so mereli the sheppards,
so mereli the sheppards ther pipes can blow,
ther pipes can blow.

SHEPHERDS, REJOICE!
Isaac Watts, 1674–1748
The most famous musical setting of this text is by the American composer
William Billings (1746–1800) who is recognized as one of the first com-
posers born in the colonies. An interesting aspect of the lyrics is that the
first two stanzas are sung by the angel Gabriel. Isaac Watts was a prodigious hymn writer and has been called the father of English hymnody. Ill
health forced an early retirement from the pastorate of Mark Lane Chapel
in London, but he continued to be active in the life of the congregation. In
addition to hymns such as *When I Survey the Wondrous Cross, O God, Our
Help in Ages Past*, and *My Shepherd Will Supply My Need*, Watts wrote a
complete versification of the Psalms and books on logic.

'Shepherds, rejoice! Lift up your eyes,
    And send your fears away;
News from the region of the skies;
    Salvation's born today!'

'Jesus, the God whom angels fear,
    Comes down to dwell with you;
Today he makes his entrance here,
    But not as monarchs do.'

Thus Gabriel sang, and straight around
    The heavenly armies throng;
They tune their harps to lofty sound
    And thus conclude the song:

'Glory to God that reigns above,
    Let peace surround the earth;
Mortals shall know their Maker's love
    At their Redeemer's birth.'

Lord! And shall angels have their songs
    And men no tunes to raise?
O may we lose these useless tongues
    When they forget to praise!

'Glory to God that reigns above,
    That pitied us forlorn!'
We join to sing our Maker's love,
    For there's a Saviour born.

WATT'S CRADLE HYMN
Isaac Watts, 1674–1748
This *Cradle Hymn* by Isaac Watts was first published in his *Moral Songs* (1706)—a collection of songs for children. The original has fourteen four-line stanzas. Watts is well known for his great number of crafted hymns (over 750) and his numerous books about philosophy and theology. It is ironic that this insightful and tender lullaby was written by a man who never had children of his own.

Hush! My dear, lie still and slumber;
    Holy angels guard thy bed!
Heav'nly blessings without number
    Gently falling on thy head.
Sleep, my babe; thy food and raiment,
    House and home thy friends provide:
All without thy care or payment,
    All thy wants are well supplied.

How much better thou'rt attended
    Than the Son of God could be
When from heaven he descended
    And became a child like thee!
Soft and easy is thy cradle,
    Coarse and hard thy Saviour lay
When his birth-place was a stable
    And his softest bed was hay.

Was there nothing but a manger
    Cursed sinners could afford
To receive the heav'nly stranger?
    Did they thus affront their Lord?
Soft! My child; I did not chide thee,
    Though my sing might sound too hard:
'Tis thy mother sits beside thee,
    And her arms shall be thy guard.

See the kindly shepherds round him,
    Telling wonders from the sky!
Where they sought him, there they found him,
    With his Virgin Mother nigh.
See the lovely Babe addressing:
    Lovely Infant, how he smiled!
When he wept, the mother's blessing
    Soothed and hushed the Holy Child.

Lo! He slumbers in his manger,
    Where the hornéd oxen fed;
Peace, my darling, here's no danger,
    Here's no ox a-near thy bed.
May'st thou live to know and fear him,
    Trust and love him all thy days;
Then go dwell for ever near him,
    See his face and sing his praise!

ONCE IN ROYAL DAVID'S CITY
Cecil Frances Alexander, 1823–1895
Cecil Frances Alexander was born in Dublin, Ireland. She married the Rev.
William Alexander who became archbishop of Armagh and later primate of
all Ireland. She wrote over four hundred hymns, of which *All Things Bright
and Beautiful* is perhaps the best known. She reportedly wrote this carol for
her godchildren when they complained that their Bible lessons were dreary.
This carol, which has become the traditional opening for the Christmas
Eve *Lessons and Carols Service* from King's College, Cambridge, was intended and written as a carol for children. It was first published in 1848 in
Hymns for Little Children, a collection of songs that went through more than
one hundred English editions. The subtle, yet straightforward, Biblical
allusions and promise of heaven make it a favorite for all ages.

Once in royal David's city stood a lowly cattle shed,
Where a mother laid her baby in a manger for his bed:
 Mary was that mother mild,
 Jesus Christ her little child.

He came down to earth from heaven who is God and Lord of all,
And his shelter was a stable, and his cradle was a stall:
 With the poor, and mean, and lowly,
 Lived on earth our Savior holy.

And through all his wondrous childhood he would honor and obey,
Love and watch the lowly maiden in whose gentle arms, he lay:
 Christian children all must be
 Mild, obedient, good as he.

And our eyes at last shall see him, through his own redeeming love;
For that child so dear and gentle is our Lord in heav'n above,
 And he leads his children on
 To the place where he is gone.

Not in that poor lowly stable, with the oxen standing by,
We shall see him, but in heaven, set at God's right hand on high;
 When like stars his children crowned
 All in white shall wait around.

GOOD CHRISTIAN MEN, REJOICE
In Dulci Jubilo
Medieval Latin
Translated by John Mason Neale, 1818–1866
John Mason Neale's translation of *In Dulci Milo* is more a translation of the German version than it is of the Latin. In addition to the Latin and German versions, there also exists a macaronic text that is a mixture of the German and Latin. The original Latin version was probably written by a Dominican monk named Heinrich Suso (1300–1365). Suso was the son of a Crusader who had entered a monastery in the Rhine. As he lay ill one night, he had a vision of a host of angels coming to him in a heavenly dance. The lead Angel took him by the hand and sang to him a carol of the Christ Child. It was this carol that he wrote down. Neale's version of the carol retains all of the joyous nature of the original but it also manages to tighten the theological elements of the text in conformity to Scripture.

Good Christian men, rejoice,
With heart and soul and voice!

Give ye heed to what we say:
    News! News!
Jesus Christ is born today.
Ox and ass before Him bow,
And he is in the manger now:
Christ is born today!
    Christ is born today!

Good Christian men, rejoice,
With heart and soul and voice!
Now ye hear of endless bliss:
    Joy! Joy!
Jesus Christ was born for this!
He hath oped the heavenly door,
And man is blessed for evermore.
Christ was born for this!
    Christ was born for this!

Good Christian men, rejoice,
With heart and soul and voice!
Now ye need not fear the grave:
    Peace! Peace!
Jesus Christ was born to save;
Calls you one, and calls you all,
To gain His everlasting hall.
Christ was born to save!
    Christ was born to save!

WHAT CHILD IS THIS?
William Chatterton Dix, 1837–1898
Dix was an Englishman who was by vocation an insurance executive and by avocation a poet. It is unknown who paired his 1865 lyrics of *What Child is This?* to *Greensleeves*, one of the most beloved melodies from the sixteenth century. This haunting music was probably written in the latter half of the 1500's and was famous enough to garner a specific mention in a Shakespearean play. Unfortunately, many modern editions of this carol in hymnals leave out the words to the chorus for verse two and three that specifically remind the singer of the purpose of Christ's incarnation.

What child is this, who, laid to rest
    On Mary's lap, is sleeping?
Whom angels greet with anthems sweet,
    While shepherds watch are keeping?
This, this is Christ the King,
    Whom shepherds guard and angels sing:
Haste, haste to bring him laud,
    The Babe, the Son of Mary!

Why lies he in such mean estate
    Where ox and ass are feeding?
Good Christian cheer for sinners here
    The Silent Word is pleading.
Nails, spear shall pierce him through
    The cross be borne for me for you.
Hail, hail the Word made flesh,
    The Babe, the Son of Mary!

So bring Him incense, gold, & myrrh,
    Come peasant king to own Him,
The King of kings, salvation brings,
    Let loving hearts enthrone Him.
Raise, raise the song on high,
    The Virgin sings her lullaby:
Joy, joy, for Christ is born,
    The Babe, the Son of Mary!

ALL MY HEART THIS NIGHT REJOICES
Frölich soll mein Herze springen
Paul Gerhardt, 1607–1676
Translated by Catherine Winkworth, 1827–1878
This carol was written during a difficult period in Paul Gerhardt's life.
Soon after he had been ejected from his pastorate for political reasons, his
wife and four children died. He went with his one remaining child to a
small parish in Luebben, Germany, where he continued his preaching and
hymn writing until his death in 1676. Despite this period of hardships,
Gerhardt was still able to write about a rejoicing heart. The only hint of his
struggles occurs in verses five and seven in which he writes of being freed
"from all the ills that grieve you" and of "that joy which can vanish never."
The overall triumphant tone is a product of a deep and trusting faith from
one of Germany's greatest hymn writers.

All my heart this night rejoices
    As I hear
    Far and near
Sweetest angel voices,

"Christ is born," Their choirs are singing
   Till the air
   Ev'rywhere
Now with joy is ringing.

Forth today the Conqueror goeth,
   Who the foe,
   Sin and woe,
Death and hell, o'erthroweth.
God is man, man to deliver;
   His dear Son
   Now is one
With our blood forever.

Shall we still dread God's displeasure,
   Who, to save,
   Freely gave
His most cherished Treasure?
To redeem us, he hath given
   His own Son
   From the throne
Of his might in heaven.

He becomes the Lamb that taketh
   Sin away
   And for aye
Full atonement maketh.
For our life his own he tenders;

And our race,
   By his grace,
Meet for glory renders.

Hark! A voice from yonder manger,
   Soft and sweet,
   Doth entreat:
"Flee from woe and danger.
 Brethren, from all ills that grieve you,
   You are freed;
   All you need
I will surely give you."

Come, then, let us hasten yonder;
   Here let all,
   Great and small,
Kneel in awe and wonder.
Love him who with love is yearning;
   Hail the star
   That from far,
Bright with hope is burning.

Dearest Lord, thee will I cherish.
   Though my breath
   Fail in death,
Yet I shall not perish,
But with thee abide forever

There on high,
In that joy
Which can vanish never.

HOW LOVELY SHINES THE MORNING STAR!
Wie Schön leuchtet der morgenstern
Philipp Nicolai, 1556–1608
Composite translation
Philipp Nicolai served as a Lutheran pastor in a church in Unna when a
terrible pestilence swept through his village. The plague claimed over 1,300
victims and struck terror into the hearts of the villagers. As many as thirty
burials took place a day in the churchyard next to the parsonage. It was one
morning when the tragedy and distress weighed especially heavy on him
that Nicolai began to write the words and music to this hymn, describing
the joys of heaven and the Savior's love. It is known as the queen of
chorales and was used by Felix Mendelssohn in his *Christus* and was harmo-
nized by J. S. Bach.

How lovely shines the Morning Star!
The nations see and hail afar
The light in Judah shining.
Thou David's son of Jacob's race,
My bridegroom and my King of grace,
For thee my heart is pining.
Lowly, holy
Great and glorious,
Thou victorious

Prince of graces,
    Filling all the heav'nly places.

Now richly to my waiting heart,
O thou, my God, deign to Impart
    The grace of love undying.
In thy blest body let me be,
E'en as the branch is in the tree,
    Thy life my life supplying.
        Sighing, crying,
    For the savor
    Of thy favor;
Resting never
    Till I rest in thee forever.

Thou, mighty Father, in thy Son
Didst love me ere thou hadst begun
    This ancient world's foundation.
Thy Son hath made a friend of me,
And when in spirit him I see,
    I joy in tribulation.
        What bliss is this!
    He that liveth
    To me giveth
Life forever,
    Nothing me from him can sever.

FROM HEAVEN ABOVE TO EARTH I COME
Vom Himmel hoch do komm ich her
Martin Luther, 1483–1546
Translated by Catherine Winkworth, 1827–78
Although this carol is internationally recognized as one of the two most famous Christmas songs from Germany, it remains virtually unknown in twentieth century English speaking countries. *Von Himmel hoch* represents Martin Luther's limited output of Christmas carols. Despite the fact that he translated several carols from Latin into German, this remains his only completely original carol. It is likely that Luther wrote this carol for a Christmas Eve ceremony that included Luther's son, Hans. Seven verses were sung by a man dressed as an angel, and the remaining fifteen verses were sung in response by children. The verses were published in 1535 and then again in 1539 with a different tune. There have been 15 to 20 different attempts at translation, with Catherine Winkworth's as the best effort; however, this carol has suffered in translation, which perhaps explains its anonymity in English.

"From heaven above to earth I come,
    To bear good news to every home;
Glad tidings of great joy I bring,
    Whereof I now will say and sing,

"'To you this night is born a Child
    Of Mary, chosen mother mild;'
This little Child, of lowly birth,
    Shall be the joy of all your earth.

" 'Tis Christ our God, who far on high
　　Hath heard your sad and bitter cry
Himself will your salvation be;
　　Himself from sin will make you free."

Welcome to earth, Thou noble Guest,
　　Through whom even wicked men are blest!
Thou com'st to share our misery;
　　What can we render, Lord, to Thee?

Were earth a thousand times as fair,
　　Beset with gold and jewels rare,
She yet were far too poor to be
　　A narrow cradle, Lord, for Thee.

Ah! Dearest Jesus, Holy Child,
　　Make Thee a bed, soft, undefiled,
Within my heart, that it may be
　　A quiet chamber kept for Thee.

My heart for very joy doth leap;
　　My lips no more can silence keep;
I too must raise with joyful tongue
　　That sweetest ancient cradle song,

"Glory to God in highest heaven,
　　Who unto man His Son hath given!

While angels sing with pious mirth
A glad New Year to all on earth.

SEE, AMID THE WINTER'S SNOW

Edward Caswall, 1814–1878

Edward Caswall was an Anglican priest who eventually joined the Roman Catholic Church under the influence of John Henry Newman. This hymn was published not long after his conversion in a volume of *Easy Hymn Tunes* in 1851. It is beautiful in its simplicity, solemnity, and its exalted language.

See, amid the winter's snow,
Born for us on earth below,
See the tender Lamb appears,
Promised from eternal years.

Hail, thou ever-blessed morn!
Hail, redemption's happy dawn!
Sing through all Jerusalem,
Christ is born in Bethlehem.

Lo, within a manger lies
He who built the starry skies:
He who, throned in height sublime,
Sits amid the cherubim.

Say, ye holy shepherds, say
What's your joyful news today?

Wherefore have ye left your sheep
   On the lonely mountain steep?

"As we watched at dead of night,
   Lo, we saw a wondrous light;
Angels singing, 'Peace on earth,'
   Told us of the Savior's birth."

Sacred infant, all divine,
   What a tender love was thine,
Thus to come from highest bliss
   Down to such a world as this!

Teach, O teach us, holy child,
   By thy face so meek and mild,
Teach us to resemble thee,
   In thy sweet humility.

VERBUM CARO
15th century English, Anonymous

Verbum caro factum est; Habitavit in nobis.
Alleluia Alleluia.
Nobum fecit Doninus Salutare suum.
Prope invocavit me Patermeus es tu.

The Word was made flesh And dwelt among us.
Alleluia. Alleluia.
The Lord has made known His salvation.
Nigh to me, he called unto me, Thou art my Father.

HARK THE HERALD ANGELS SING
Charles Wesley, 1707–1788
This beloved Christmas carol was composed in 1739, the year following Charles Wesley's conversion to Christianity. Wesley was a prolific hymn writer of many enduring texts. The familiar opening lines of *Hark the Herald Angels Sing* originally were: "Hark! How all the Welkin rings, Glory to the King of Kings." Further changes were made to the end of the first stanza from: "Universal nature say, Christ the Lord is born today" to: "With the angelic hosts proclaim, Christ is born in Bethlehem. "The hymn had been in use for one hundred and twenty years before it was finally paired with the familiar tune composed by Felix Mendelssohn. Mendelssohn had written a piece of music to commemorate the anniversary of the discovery of printing and said that the piece "will never do to sacred words. There must be a national and merry subject found out, to which the soldier-like motion of the piece has some relation." Thankfully he was wrong.

JOY TO THE WORLD
From Psalm 98
Isaac Watts, 1674–1748
Isaac Watts is known as the Father of English hymnody. When he was fifteen years old, he complained to his father, a deacon at the church in

Southampton, England, that the congregational singing was listless. His father challenged him to provide better hymns for them to sing, and he did. At the age of twenty-one, Watts preached his first sermon in the Independent Church in Mark Lane, London. After his health failed, he maintained a relationship with the church but was unable to preach regularly. He began to devote more time to writing hymns, poems, and books of philosophy and theology. He was already famous for his *Hymns and Spiritual Songs*, 1707, and in 1719 his collection of psalm paraphrases was published with the title *The Psalms of David in the Language of the New Testament*. His paraphrase of the last five verse of Psalm 98 were entitled *Messiah's Coming and Kingdom*, it is more commonly known as *Joy to the World*.

ANGELS WE HAVE HEARD ON HIGH
Traditional French Carol (18th century?)
Gloria in excelsis Deo is the Latin version of "Glory to God in the highest," the words that the angels sang to the shepherds on the night of the Nativity. There is a tradition that Pope Telesphorus, who ruled as pope between about 125–136, ordained that all should sing the "Gloria in excelsis Deo" on Christmas. He wrote that: "On the birthday of the Lord, Masses should be said at night ... and the angelic hymn 'Gloria in excelsis Deo' should be said before the sacrifice." Others place the tradition of the "Gloria" response as originating in the third century. Whatever the case, *Angels We Have Heard on High* utilizes a beautiful melody to proclaim Glory to God in the highest.

O COME, ALL YE FAITHFUL
Adeste Fideles
Latin Hymn, 18th century
John Francis Wade, 1711–1786
The history of this hymn had been shrouded in mystery until the discovery
of a manuscript in 1946. The apparent author of both the words and music
of *O Come, All Ye Faithful* was a Englishman who lived and worked at the
Roman Catholic college for Englishmen at Douai in Northern France. In
addition to teaching music, Wade's work included the job of copying music
for Catholic institutions and families in various places. He wrote the hymn
in Latin in 1744, and an edition of his manuscript appeared in Lisbon,
Portugal, and in the Portuguese embassy in London in the 1750's. Since
then, the carol has been translated into more than one hundred and
twenty-five languages including over fifty versions in English. By far the
most popular English version is by Frederick Oakley (1802–1880). Oakley
was educated at Christ Church, Oxford, where he won special honors in
Latin. There are eight verses in the original version, but only half of those
are usually sung.

O LITTLE TOWN OF BETHLEHEM
Phillips Brooks, 1835–1893
After Phillips Brooks graduated from Harvard University, he unsuccessfully
tried teaching at the Boston Latin School. Subsequent studies at the
Episcopal Theological Seminary at Alexandria, Virginia, proved to be much
more in line with his gifts. After serving as rector of the Holy Trinity
Church in Philadelphia for a few years, he left on a year-long travel sabbat-
ical that included a trip to the Holy Land. On Sunday, December 24, 1865,
he traveled from Jerusalem to Bethlehem by horseback and saw the field of

the Shepherds and attended a five hour Christmas Eve service in the Church of the Nativity. It was from that experience that he wrote *O Little Town of Bethlehem* two years later. Brooks went on to serve as the Episcopal Bishop of Massachusetts and was a well respected and well-known orator, author, and minister. The tune for this carol was written by Brooks' friend and organist in Philadelphia, Lewis H. Redner (1831–1908) who wrote the melody in a burst of inspiration the night before a Christmas program.

GOD REST YE MERRY, GENTLEMEN
English Traditional
There is frequently a misunderstanding concerning the opening lines of this traditional English carol. "God rest ye merry, Gentlemen" means "God keep you in good spirits, gentlemen;" however, the comma is sometimes misplaced and gives the meaning "God give you rest, merry-making gentlemen." In addition to being one of England's favorite carols, this piece also has the distinction of playing a role in literature. *God Rest Ye Merry, Gentlemen* is the carol from *A Christmas Carol* by Charles Dickens (1812–1870). Early in the story, a London street lad serenaded Scrooge with these lines while he was in the counting house. These words and sentiment caused Scrooge to ferociously seize "the ruler with such energy of action that the singer fled in terror." Despite Scrooge's response, there is something irrepressible about this carol and its tidings of comfort and joy.

O HOLY NIGHT!
Cantique de Noël
M. Placide Cappeau de Roquemaure, 1808–1877
Translated by John S. Dwight, 1813–1893
Not much is known about the author of *O Holy Night*, Placide Cappeau,

other than this work appears to have been at the request of his parish priest. The priest suggested that Cappeau, a commissionaire of wines and an occasional poet, write a Christmas poem and take it to the famous Parisian composer Adolphe Adam (1803–1856). Adam had gained a reputation in the music world for his ballet, *Giselle*. Half way to Paris on December 3, 1847, Cappeau wrote the lyrics in a coach. Adams completed the music in time for a premier performance at the Midnight Mass on Christmas Eve. The most famous story associated with this song occurred during the Franco-Prussian War of 1870–1871. French and German troops were facing each other in trenches outside the besieged city of Paris. On Christmas Eve, a French soldier suddenly jumped from the trench and started to sing *Cantique de Noël*, while the Germans quietly watched in astonishment. At the conclusion of the song, the ensuing silence was broken by a tall German soldier who sang a rendition of Martin Luther's German hymn, *From Heaven Above to Earth I Come*.

WHILE SHEPHERDS WATCHED THEIR FLOCKS BY NIGHT
Luke 2:8–14
Nahum Tate, 1652–1715
Irish-born Nahum Tate set out to provide a Christian hymnody for the Church distinct from the practice of Psalm singing. His result was *While Shepherds Watched Their Flocks By Night* and fifteen other hymns paraphrased from the New Testament that he published with Nicholas Brady as *The New Version of the Psalms of David (1700)*. This work and others like it did much to effect the change from psalm to hymn singing in Britain. Tate was a recognized talent, and was named poet laureate of England in 1692. In 1702 he was appointed royal historiographer and gained lasting

success with his version of *King Lear.* His work, complete with a happy ending, was more popular than Shakespeare's tragedy for over a century and a half.

AWAY IN A MANGER
Anonymous, ca. 1884
Away in a Manger is often referred to Martin Luther's *Cradle Hymn* and even reputable hymnals and other publications have made that assertion. However, it now seems ludicrous that a German hymn written 400 years before would finally service in English in American sources in the late 1800's. Although the hymn writer remains a mystery, it has been fairly accurately ascertained that the hymn was written among the colony of German Lutherans in Pennsylvania. This story only accounts for the first two verses. The third verse was added sometime later by yet another anonymous source. There have also been several misleading and confusing stories surrounding the composition of the most common tune (there have been over forty melodies associated with the text). The leading theory is that James R. Murray (1841–c. 1904) wrote the music for an 1887 publication but refused credit, perhaps hoping that the suggestion of Luther's authorship of text and tune would increase the melody's popularity.

ANGELS FROM THE REALMS OF GLORY
James Montgomery, 1771–1854
James Montgomery was born to a devout peasant family in Ayrshire, Scotland. He studied for the ministry, but a greater interest in writing poetry caused him to leave school. He eventually wrote over four hundred hymns. The text for *Angels From the Realms of Glory* was first published on

December 24, 1816 in *The Sheffield Iris*, a journal that Montgomery edited. All of his hymns are evidence of a wide knowledge of Scripture, and this example is no different. In the four stanzas reproduced in modern hymnals, Montgomery succinctly tells of the angels, shepherds, Wise Men, and the prophets who were waiting for the consolation of Israel. Writing about this hymn, one writer said, "For comprehensiveness, appropriateness of expression, force and elevation of sentiment, it may challenge comparison with any hymn that was ever written, in any language or country."

SILENT NIGHT, HOLY NIGHT
Stille Nacht, heilige Nacht
Joseph Mohr, 1792–1848
The popularity of *Silent Night* cannot be questioned; it has been translated into more than ninety languages and dialects. However, there has been much lore and legend surrounding the composition of this quintessential Christmas carol. Franz Gruber (1787–1863), the composer of the tune, gives the definitive version of the story in a signed statement issued by him: "It was on December 24 of the year 1818 when Joseph Mohr, then assistant pastor of the newly established St. Nicholas' parish church in Oberndorf, handed to Franz Gruber, who was attending to the duties of organist (and was at the same time a schoolmaster in Arnsdorf) a poem, with the request that he write for it a suitable melody arranged for two solo voices, chorus, and a guitar accompaniment. On that very same evening the latter, in fulfillment of this request made to him as a music expert, handed to the pastor his simple composition, which was thereupon immediately performed on that holy night of Christmas Eve and received with all acclaim ... Franz Gruber, Town Parish Choir Director and Organist, Hallein, December 30, 1854."

CHRISTMAS BALLADS AND VERSE

I HEARD THE BELLS ON CHRISTMAS DAY
Henry W. Longfellow, 1824–1884
Longfellow wrote this poem (which he called "Christmas Bells") on
December 25, 1863—just six months after the Battle of Gettysburg. It
reflects the anxiety and weariness of millions of Americans during the War
Between the States. However, the desire for peace echoed in the song is not
just the temporal cease of conflict, but the everlasting peace of a conquer-
ing King who has vanquished that which is wrong.

I heard the bells on Christmas Day
Their old, familiar carols play,
    And wild and sweet
    The words repeat
Of peace on earth, good will to men!

I thought how, as the day had come,
The belfries of all Christendom
    Had rolled along
    The unbroken song
Of peace on earth, good will to men!

And in despair I bowed my head:
"There is no peace on earth," I said,
    "For hate is strong
    And mocks the song
Of peace on earth, good will to men!

Then pealed the bells more loud and deep:
"God is not dead; nor doth he sleep!
    The wrong shall fail,
    The right prevail,
With peace on earth, good will to men!"

JOLLY WAT
Anonymous
The rugged good nature of the jolly shepherd is captured in this traditional
English Medieval ballad.

Can I not sing but 'Hoy',
Whan the joly shepard made so much joy?

I

The shepard upon a hill he sat;
He had on him his tabard and his hat,
His tarbox, his pipe, and his flagat;
His name was called Joly Joly Wat,
For he was a gud herdes boy.
        Ut hoy!
    For in his pipe he made so much joy.

II

The shepard upon a hill was laid;
His dog unto his girdell was taid;
He had not slept but a litill braid;

But *'Gloria in excelsis'* was to him said.
>> Ut hoy!
> For in his pipe he made so much joy.

The shepard kon ahill he stode;
Round about him his shepe they yode;
He put his hond under his hode,
He saw a star as rede as blode.
>> Ut hoy!
> For in his pipe he made so much joy.

IV

The shepard said anon right,
'I will go see yon ferly sight,
Whereas the angel singeth on hight,
And the star that shineth so bright.'
>> Ut hoy!
> For in his pipe he made so much joy.

V

'Now farewell, Mall, and also Will!
For my love go ye all still
Unto I cum again you till,
And evermore, Will, ring well thy bell.'
>> Ut hoy!
> For in his pipe he made so much joy.

VI

'Now must I go there Crist was born;
Farewell! I cum again to-morn.
Dog, kepe well my shepe fro the corn,
And warn well "Warroke" when I blow my horn!'
      Ut hoy!
   For in his pipe he made so much joy.

VII

Whan Wat to Bedlem cumen was
He swet, he had gone faster than a pace;
He found Jesu in a simpell place,
Betwen an ox but and an asse.
      Ut hoy!
   For in his pipe he made so much joy.

VIII

'Jesu, I offer to thee here my pipe,
My skirt, my tar-box, and my scrip;
Home to my felowes now will I skip,
And also look unto my shepe.'
      Ut hoy!
For in his pipe he made so much joy.

IX

'Now faresell, mine owne herdesman Wat!'—
'Yea, for God, lady, even so I hat;
Lull well Jesu in thy lat,

And farewell, Joseph, with thy round cap!'
    Ut hoy!
  For in his pipe he made so much joy.

       X
Now may I well both hope and sing,
for I have bene at Cristes bering;
Home to my felowes now will I fling.
Crist of heven to his bliss us bring!'
    Ut hoy!
  For in his pipe he made so much joy.

A MEDITATION FOR CHRISTMAS
Selwyn Image, 1849–1930
Born in Sussex, England, Selwyn Image pursued dual careers in artistic
design and the clergy. He was educated at Oxford where he was profoundly
affected by the lectures of art critic and historian, John Ruskin. Image
became a curate, but he resigned in 1882 to concentrate entirely on illustra-
tion and design. He designed for embroidery, mosaics, and stained glass,
and he was Professor of Fine Arts at Oxford from 1910–1916.

Consider, O my soul, what morn is this!
  Whereon the eternal Lord of all things made,
For us, poor mortals, and our endless bliss,
  Came down from heaven; and, in a manger laid,
  The first, rich, offerings of our ransom paid:
Consider, O my soul, what morn is this!

Consider what estate of fearful woe
    Had then been ours, had He refused this birth;
Form sin to sin toss'd vainly to and fro,
    Hell's playthings, o'er a doom'd and helpless earth!
    Had He from us withheld His priceless worth,
Consider man's estate of fearful woe!

Consider to what joys He bids thee rise,
    Who comes, Himself, life's bitter cup to drain!
Ah! look on this sweet Child, whose innocent eyes,
    Ere all be done, shall close in mortal pain,
    That thou at last Love's Kingdom may'st attain:
Consider to what joys He bids thee rise!

Consider all this wonder, O my soul;
    And in thine inmost shrine make music sweet!
Yea, let the world, from furthest pole to pole,
    Join in thy praises this dread birth to greet-,
    Kneeling to kiss thy Saviour's infant feet!
Consider all this wonder, O my soul!

A CHRISTMAS RHYME
G. K. Chesterton, 1874–1936
Taking great glee in Christmas, the prolific author and reformer, G. K. Chesterton wrote voluminously on the subject. As he grew older, his appreciation for the mystery of Christmas became even greater as is evidenced in this rich excerpt from his wide canon of Yuletide verse.

When God was born in Bethlehem
He drank the milk of man.
And Mary asking "Is it fit?"
He bowed and clung and whispered it.
"Mother, I say a dreadful thing
Save for my savage and swift coming
At last, even mortal mothers would
Have wearied of all motherhood,
When the babe was but a span."

When God was gone through Galilee,
The water turned to wine,
They questioned because of the crimson freak,
He said, "Because all wine grows weak,
Yea, man grows colder than a cow,
They turn the wine to water now.
Alone I lift the feasting face,
For Bacchus, on the hills of Thrace,
Is weary of the vine."

When God was in Jerusalem,
The wine was turned to blood.
They wept. He said, "Without this strife
Death had grown even as dull as life.
The sages stare and can but spy
Blue devils in the good blue sky,
But only God in agony

Can look on all good things that be,
And see that they are good."

Then do we bid a blessing down
On milk and blood and wine.
All huge and humble things we bless,
For a man's great thought is grown a guess,
And woman's smile is grown a snare,
And power is in the creeds of fear,
And praise is on the thrones of theft,
And there are no things human left,
But those He made divine.

PRAYERS FOR CHRISTMAS

THE NATIVITY OF OUR LORD: CHRISTMAS DAY
Book of Common Prayer, 1789
O God, who makest us glad with the yearly remembrance of the birth of
thy only Son Jesus Christ: Grant that as we joyfully receive him for our
Redeemer, so we may with sure confidence behold him when he shall come
to be our Judge; who liveth and reigneth with thee and the Holy Ghost,
one God, world without end. *Amen.*

PRAYER FOR CHRISTMAS DAY
Book of Common Prayer, 1789
O God,
    who hast caused this holy night
        to shine with the illumination of the true Light:
Grant us, we beseech thee,
    that as we have known the mystery of that Light upon earth,
    so may we also perfectly enjoy him in heaven;
where with thee and the Holy Spirit he liveth and reigneth,
    one God, in glory everlasting. *Amen.*

A CHRISTMAS PRAYER
Book of Common Prayer, 1789
Almighty God,
    who hast given us thy only-begotten Son
        to take our nature upon him
        and as at this time to be born of a pure virgin:

Grant that we, being regenerate
    and made thy children by adoption and grace,
may daily be renewed by thy Holy Spirit;
through the same our Lord Jesus Christ,
    who liveth and reigneth with thee
    and the same Spirit ever,
one God, world without end. *Amen.*

PRAYER FOR THE DAY OF JOY
Henry van Dyke (1852–1933)
The day of joy returns Father in Heaven, and crowns another year with peace and good will. Help us rightly to remember the birth of Jesus, that we may share in the song of the angels, the gladness of the shepherds, and the worship of the wise men. Close the doors of hate and open the doors of love all over the world. Let kindness come with every gift and good desires with every greeting. Deliver us from evil, by the blessing that Christ brings, and teach us to be merry with clean hearts. May the Christmas morning make us happy to be Thy children, and the Christmas evening bring us to our bed with grateful thoughts, forgiving and forgiven, for Jesus sake. *Amen.*

DAILY READINGS FOR CHRISTMAS

CHRISTMAS MORNING
John 1: 1-37 — St. John unfolds the great mystery of the Incarnation—the coming of the Lamb of God.

CHRISTMAS EVENING
Revelation 5:1-14 — St. John reveals the glory of the completed work of Christ—the exalted Lamb of God.

St. Nicholas and the Origins of Christmas Traditions

Nicholas of Myra (c. 288–354), the fourth century pastor who inspired the tradition of Santa Claus, may not have lived at the North Pole or traveled by reindeer and sleigh but he certainly was a paradigm of graciousness, generosity, and Christian charity. His great love and concern for children drew him into a crusade that ultimately resulted in protective Imperial statutes that remained in place in Byzantium for more than a thousand years.

Though little is known of his childhood, he was probably born to wealthy parents at Patara in Lycia, a Roman province of Asia Minor. As a young man noted for his piety, judiciousness, and charity, he was chosen bishop of the then rundown diocese of Myra. There he became gained renown for his personal holiness, evangelistic zeal, and pastoral compassion.

Early Byzantine histories reported that he suffered imprisonment and made a famous profession of faith during the persecution of Diocletian. He was also reputedly present at the Council of Nicaea, where he forthrightly condemned there heresy of Arianism—one story holds that he actually slapped the heretic Arius.

But it was his love for and care of children that gained him his greatest renown. Though much of what we know about his charitable work on behalf of the poor, the despised, and the rejected has been distorted by legend and lore over the centuries, it is evident that he was a particular champion of the downtrodden, bestowing upon them gifts as tokens of the grace and mercy of the Gospel.

One legend tells of how a citizen of Patara lost his fortune, and because he could not raise dowries for his three young daughters, he was going to give them over to prostitution. After hearing this, Nicholas took a small bag of gold and threw it through the window of the man's house on the eve of the feast of Christ's Nativity. The eldest girl was married with it as her dowry. He performed the same gracious service for each of the other girls on each of the succeeding nights. The three purses, portrayed in art with the saint, were thought to be the origin of the pawnbroker's symbol of three gold balls.

But they were also the inspiration for Christians to begin the habit of gift giving during each of the twelve days of Christmas—from December 25 until Epiphany on January 6.

In yet another legend, Nicholas saved several youngsters from certain death when he pulled them from a deep vat of vinegar brine-again, on the feast of the Nativity. Ever afterward, Christians remembered the day by giving one another the gift of large crisp pickles.

The popular cultural representation of St. Nicholas as Father Christmas or Santa Claus, though drawing on a number of such legends, was based primarily on a the Dutch custom of giving children presents—slipping fruits, nuts, and little toys into shoes or stockings drying along the warm hearthside—on his feast day, December 6. Throughout the rest of Europe during the middle ages, that day was marked by festively decorating homes and by a sumptuous feast that interrupted the general fasting of Advent. And in Scandanavia it was celebrated as a day of visitation, when the elders of all the remote country churches would bundle themselves in their thick furs and drive their sleighs laden with gift pastries through the snowy land-scape to every home within the parish.

Through the centuries, the traditions associated with Nicholas have proven to be an inducement to steer clear of the twin pitfalls and pratfalls of materialism and asceticism. In the midst of the whirling change of the modern world, we need those traditions more than ever. The efficacy of tradition to offer stability, continuity, and guidance is indubitable. Connections to the past are the only sure leads to the future. Thus the realm of tradition is not just the concern of historians and social scientists. It is not the lonely domain of political prognosticators and ivory tower academics. It is the very stuff of life. And, in fact, it is the very stuff of faith. Indeed, the Bible put a heavy emphasis on historical awareness—not at all surprising considering the fact that the vast proportion of its own contents record the dealings of God with men and nations throughout the ages.

Again and again that stress is evident in the Scriptures. God calls upon His people to remember: He calls on them to remember the bondage, oppression, and deliverance of Egypt; He calls on them to remember the splendor, strength, and devotion of the Davidic Kingdom; He calls on them to remember the valor, forthrightness, and holiness of the prophets; He calls on them to remember the glories of creation, the devastation of the flood, the judgment of the great apostasies, the miraculous events of the exodus, the anguish of the desert wanderings, the grief of the Babylonian exile, the responsibility of the restoration, the sanctity of the Lord's Day, the graciousness of the commandments, and the ultimate victory of the cross; He calls on them to remember the lives and witness of all those who have gone before in faith—forefathers, fathers, patriarchs, prophets, apostles, preachers, evangelists, martyrs, confessors, ascetics, and every righteous spirit made pure in Christ. Indeed, he believed that remembrance and forgetfulness were the measuring rods of faithfulness throughout the entire canon of Scripture—that is why the Bible makes it plain that there are only two kinds of people in the world: effectual doers and forgetful hearers.

We are enamoured of progress. We are living at a time when things shiny and new are prized far above things old and timeworn. For most of us, tradition is little more than a quirky and nostalgic sentimentalism. It is hardly more than the droning, monotonous succession of obsolete notions, anachronous ideals, and antiquarian habits, sound and fury, signifying nothing. Henry Ford called an awareness of history and an appreciation for the past mere "bunk." Augustine Birrell called it "a dust heap." Guy de Maupassant dubbed it "that excitable and lying old lady." But many of the wisest of men and women through the ages have recognized that tradition is a foundation upon which all true advancement must be built—that it is in fact, the prerequisite to all genuine progress.

Stable societies must be eternally vigilant in the task of handing on their great legacy-to remember and then to inculcate that remembrance in the hearts and minds of their children. Alas, any people who did not know their own history, would simply have to endure all the same mistakes, sacrifices, and absurdities all over again.

Sadly, such lessons are very nearly lost on us in this odd to-whom-it-may-concern, instant-everything day of microwaveable meals, prefab buildings, bottom-rung bureaucracy, fit-for-the-market education, knee-jerk public misinformation, and predigested formula entertainment. Thus temporary expediencies supersede permanent exigencies.

Christmas traditions, like those that revolve around the character of Nicholas of Myra, may well be abused by modern marketers and commercial concerns. But they can also be powerful inducements to remember the things that matter most. They can be the means by which beauty, goodness, and truth come to prevail in our homes, our communities, and our land.

CHRISTMAS TRADITIONS

CHRISTMAS EVE
The night before the Feast of Christ's Nativity has always been a time of special anticipation for Christian families. The end of the Advent preparation marked a time of special feasting. There was always good food to look forward to—and the aromas of the last round of baking filled homes with delight. In addition, the special tradition of gift giving, almost universally practiced by the end of the fourth century or so, particularly excited the imaginations of children. As a result, the evening became a kind of vigil for everyone, young and old alike.

SLEIGH RIDES
Mimicking the supposed pattern of pastoral care practiced by Nicholas of Myra, the sleigh ride-particularly on Christmas Eve-gradually was woven into the joyous celebration of Christmas. Beginning in Scandanavia, spreading to Germany, England, Scotland, and finally New England, the sounds of the jingling bells, the tramping of horses through the snow, and the brisk wind through the trees became essential elements in provoking the Yuletide Spirit.

REINDEER
Scandanavian images have greatly influenced our modern vision of the traditional Christmas-from the thick fur garb of Santa to the manner of his transport. The romantic image of reindeer pulling his sleigh was grafted into our cultural vocabulary by Danish, Swedish, and Norwegian immigrants to America during the nineteenth century.

SANTA

The transformation of St. Nicholas into Santa Claus is rooted in a number of intertwined traditions, legends, and archetypes. But perhaps more than any other sources, the advertising of soft drink manufacturer Coca Cola and the holiday cartoons of New York newspaperman Thomas Nash have profoundly shaped our perception. Coca Cola's serving trays, signage, and print ads popularized the Nash caricature of a rotund, jolly, fur-draped, gift-laden, and unbidden visitor who pops down chimneys and distributes gifts to children all over the world. Alas, thus stripped of his pastoral function and parish proximity, Santa has become almost fairy-like in his mythic proportions.

ANGELS

They were the first heralds of the miraculous spectacle of the incarnation in Bethlehem two millennia ago. Not surprisingly then, representations of angels have accompanied Christmas celebrations ever since. They appear atop Christmas trees, in table top arrangements, adorning evergreen wreaths, outlined in lights along the hearthside, and astride candles and candelabras. They play a prominent role in Christmas carols, Christmas tales, and Christmas decorations. They are featured in Christmas arts, crafts, and designs. Indeed, they lend solemnity and credulity to the glory of the Yuletide season.

NATIVITY SCENES

Representative reminders of the crèche in Bethlehem have been central to the celebrations of Christians for centuries. Most of the great European cathedrals, town squares, castles, and palaces were adorned with scenes of the wise men, shepherds, and stable animals gathered around the holy family of Mary, Joseph, and the baby Jesus. Along the Mediterranean, scenes carved from olive wood were especially prized beginning in the sixth century-and so remain to this day.

CHRISTMAS GIFTS

Exchanging gifts—specially wrapped in beautiful foils and papers—were a feature of Christmas celebrations from as early as the fifth century. A reminder to everyone within the community of faith that "It is more blessed to give than to receive," the gifts well represented the character of the incarnation itself—the most glorious act of selfless giving that could every be possibly imagined. Thus, gift giving was originally conceived as an act of covenant renewal and commitment.

LITURGICAL COLORS

The colors of the Church have special symbolism throughout the year, and this fact is readily apparent during the time of Advent, Christmas, and Epiphany. Paraments are the altar cloths, pulpit cloths, and sometimes banners that proclaim the color of the Church or liturgical year. The first color of the season is the Advent color of purple. Purple is a penitential color that explains why it is also displayed during the season of Lent. Purple is the color of royalty because of its scarcity in the Ancient world. It is also the color of the robes the mocking soldiers placed on Christ before his crucifixion. Purple is used during the penitential seasons of Advent and Lent as a reminder of the sacrifice of Christ and the scorn that he endured for our salvation. Ecclesiastical purple should invoke a daily reminder of the need for all Christians to humbly give attention to a life of repentance. White is the color of purity and completeness, and is, therefore, the color appointed for such festive Sundays as Christmas and its twelve days; Epiphany

(January 6) and the first Sunday following it, which is usually observed as the Baptism of Our Lord. The incarnation of Christ as Emmanuel, God with us, as well as the culmination of God's plan for redemption are symbolized in the purity and completeness of the color white. The color red symbolizes passion and blood. As a parament, red is used during the week leading to Easter, Pentecost, and for the days set aside in honor of martyrs. The red blood of the martyrs shed in defense of the Gospel offers perpetual encouragement for God's people to be resolute in living the faith. The red of holly berries is the foreshadowing of the shed blood of Christ on our behalf. Green is the color utilized through the season of Epiphany. The coming of the Magi is a reminder of the gift of salvation that is offered not just to Jews but Gentiles as well. Green represents growth and vitality as in the spreading of the gospel to all the ends of the earth. The green of evergreens and holly branches symbolize the coming of Life in Christ during the midst of the dead Winter of our sin.

CAROLING

Carols are songs that are usually narrative and celebratory in nature with a simple spirit and often in verse form. The term carol has a varied and interesting past and is derived from several foreign words that include the idea of dancing as well as singing. It has been often mentioned that the first carol was sung by the Angels to the shepherds on the night of Christ's birth. Mary's song, the *Magnificat*, could also fit in the category of early Christmas music. The idea of caroling from one home to another seems to have started sometime during the 18th century or earlier. Carolers would visit each house of a parish on Christmas Night to sing songs of the Nativity and to call forth blessings on every home. The term *wassail* means

"Good health!" Carolers would often receive food, money, and drink for the spreading of good cheer.

BELLS

Bells are used to summon, to ring for joy and sometimes in alarm. Some early bell ringers believed that the sound of bells would frighten away evil spirits. The Church has used bells throughout the centuries to spread news of victory, death, and celebration. Some bell ringing traditions, such as change-ringing, are intricate and involved patterns of sound based on mathematical formula as well as aesthetics. Whatever the form, the pealing of bells are distinctive heralds to the Good News of Christmas.

Treats for Christmas

Winter Haven Bread Pudding

4	eggs
2	cups milk
	Pinch salt
2	teaspoons of vanilla extract
2	to 3 tablespoons Brandy (optional)
6 +	cups cubed French bread
2	teaspoons cinnamon
½	teaspoon nutmeg
½	cup of raisins
2	tablespoons of melted butter

In a large bowl whisk together the eggs, milk, salt, vanilla, and brandy. Set aside.

In a 1½ quart casserole combine the French bread, cinnamon, nutmeg, and raisins. Sprinkle the melted butter over the bread mixture. Add the egg mixture and make sure that all of the bread is moistened. Bake at 350° for 50 to 60 minutes until an inserted knife comes out clean.

Makes 6 servings.

Czech Kolaches

	Pinch sugar
¼	cup warm water
3	packages dry yeast
7	cups all-purpose flour
¾	cup sugar
1¾	teaspoon salt
¾	cup margarine
1½	cups milk
3	egg yolks beaten

In a medium bowl add a pinch of sugar to the warm water. Add the yeast and let set until bubbly. Sift the flour into a large bowl and set aside. Scald the milk. Add ¾ cup of sugar and the salt. Stir well. Add the shortening to the milk mixture and let melt. Add the milk mixture to the flour. Beat in the yeast and eggs. Beat until the dough is smooth. It should not be sticky. Sprinkle the top of the dough with a little flour, cover, and set aside in a warm place to rise until double in bulk.

Turn the dough out on a lightly floured board. Cut into small pieces and form into walnut size balls. Place on a greased baking sheet and brush with warm shortening or margarine. Let rise until almost double in size. Indent the center for filling. Fill with fruit filling. Let rise again. Bake at 400° for 8 to 10 minutes or until lightly brown. Remove from the oven and brush the edges with margarine. Cover with a cloth to cool.

Makes 5 to 6 dozen.

Slovak Kolaches

½	cup all-purpose flour
½	cup sugar
½	cup butter
1¼	cups evaporated milk
¾	cup water
¾	cup oil
½	cup sugar
2	teaspoons salt
6	egg yolks
¼	cup instant potatoes-add enough water to make mashed potatoes
3	packages yeast dissolved in another 3/4 cup water and 2 tablespoons sugar
6	to 7 cups all-purpose flour

In a small bowl mix ½ cup of flour, ½ cup of sugar, and the butter. Refrigerate the topping.

In a large bowl beat the eggs, oil, sugar, and salt. Add the warm milk, water, and potatoes. Stir in the yeast and add the flour. Let the dough rise.

Turn the dough out on a lightly floured board. Cut into small pieces and form into walnut size balls. Let rise until double in size. Indent the center for filling. Fill with fruit filling.

Sprinkle the topping over the fruit filling. Let rise after filling.

Bake at 400° for 10 minutes. Brush with butter and when cooled sprinkle confectioners' sugar on top.

Makes 5 to 6 dozen.

COTTAGE CHEESE FILLING FOR KOLACHES

1½   cups cottage cheese drained
¼   cup sugar
1   tablespoon lemon juice
1   egg beaten
¼   cup chopped nuts optional
½   cup raisins

In a medium bowl combine all of the ingredients and mix well.
   Variation: Use ½ teaspoon vanilla extract, cinnamon and raisins instead of nuts.

OTHER SUGGESTED KOLACHE FILLINGS

Cherry pie filling
Mincemeat
Thickened crushed pineapple
Prune Filling
Poppy seed
Apricot

Roast Goose with Sage and Scallion Dressing

1	cup butter
12	scallions, white and green parts only, thinly sliced
1	medium onion, chopped
1	cup chopped celery
1	small apple, coarsely chopped
6	cups coarse dry breadcrumbs
½	teaspoon salt
1	teaspoon freshly ground black pepper
2	tablespoons chopped fresh sage (or 1 tablespoon dried sage)
1	teaspoon dried thyme
2	tablespoons chopped parsley
1	12- to 14-pound goose
½	cup chicken stock
2	large eggs, lightly beaten
	Cider, for basting

In a skillet melt the butter and sauté the scallions, onion, celery, and apple for 10 minutes or until the onion is transparent and golden brown. Transfer to a large mixing bowl and add the bread crumbs, salt, pepper, and herbs. Toss to combine. Add a bit more stock if the stuffing seems too dry.

Rinse and dry the goose and season the cavity with salt and pepper. Stuff the goose loosely with the dressing and truss using trussing skewers and string. Prick the exterior of the goose all over with a sharp-tined fork to allow excess fat to escape during roasting.

Place the goose on a rack in a large, deep roasting pan, breast-side up. Roast at 450° for 15 minutes. Reduce the oven temperature to 350° and continue roasting for about 20 minutes per pound, or until the goose is very well browned and the leg joints move up and down easily. During the roasting time remove any fat that accumulates in the pan and baste with cider.

When the goose is done, remove it to a board and let it rest, loosely covered with aluminum foil, for 30 minutes before carving. Make the gravy while the goose is resting.

Makes 8 to 10 servings.

Goose Gravy

¼   cup goose fat
¼   cup all-purpose flour
4   cups chicken stock
    Pan drippings and scrapings
    Salt and freshly ground black pepper to taste

When removing the goose fat from the pan during roasting, reserve 1/4 cup. In a heavy saucepan heat the goose fat, over medium heat. Slowly stir in the flour. Cook slowly, stirring frequently, until a brown roux has formed. Add the chicken stock a cup at a time, stirring constantly. Simmer about 5 to 7 minutes or until the flour is cooked and the gravy is thickened.

When the goose comes out of the pan, pour off the fat, then pour off the remaining drippings and any scraped browned bits from the pan into the gravy. Stir to blend thoroughly and season with salt and pepper to taste.

Makes 6 to 8 servings.

Plum Pudding

2	cups currants, coarsely chopped
2	cups craisins (dried cranberries) or raisins, coarsely chopped
½	cup blanched almonds, chopped
1	teaspoon grated nutmeg
1	teaspoon ground cinnamon
1	teaspoon allspice
1	cup all-purpose flour
1	teaspoon salt
1	pound shortening
12	ounces fresh brown breadcrumbs
1⅓	cups brown sugar
8	eggs, beaten
½	cup brandy
½	cup sherry
½	cup milk
	Brandy Butter (recipe follows)

In a large bowl mix the chopped currants, craisins, and almonds with the spices. (You may add chopped candied fruits to taste at this point.) Add the flour, salt, and chopped almonds and mix well. Work in the breadcrumbs, shortening, and brown sugar until thoroughly mixed together.

In a separate bowl beat the eggs, then add to pudding mixture. Add the brandy, sherry, and milk, stirring until thoroughly mixed. Cover and refrigerate overnight.

In the morning, pour the mixture into one very large or two small well buttered pudding basins, cover with greased wax paper and cloth, and secure cloth with rubber band or twine. Set the basin in a large open roasting pan filled about three-fourths of the way up the sides of the basin with boiling water. Steam the pudding in this way, adding hot water as necessary, for eight hours.

Remove the wet cloths and cover the pudding with fresh greased paper and cloths, secured with rubber bands or twine. Store in a cool, dark place such as the refrigerator for at least four weeks.

On Christmas morning, steam the pudding an additional 2 hours. Unmold and serve with brandy butter.

Brandy Butter

½   cup unsalted butter, softened
1   cup confectioner's sugar
½   cup brandy

In a medium bowl beat the butter until creamy. Gradually beat in the confectioner's sugar until fluffy. Add the brandy and mix thoroughly.

Epiphany

*T*he celebration of Epiphany is the culmination of what is traditionally called the Twelve Days of Christmas. The word literally
means "revelation" or "sudden unveiling" or "manifestation." It
commemorates the day when wise men from the East were conducted
by a miraculous star to the nativity in Bethlehem. The magi were
thus the first to comprehend that Jesus was not merely the prophetic
fulfillment of Jewish aspirations since the beginning of time. Instead,
He was the hope of the world, the light of the world, and the joy of
every man's desiring. They beheld the very glory of God that day—
for in the city of David, the Savior was born. As a result, Epiphany
is the celebration of the ultimate proclamation of good news.
Good news, indeed.

Incarnational hope hastens hence
on bud, breeze, and blossom
grieving rynds banished in lilac scents.

Hark, the Epiphany Hymn rings haste
from its loveliest biding-place.

A lavish breach of winter's curt hard sword
an ardent repudiation of death's dark pall
the out-viening sun of the Christus Lord.

Hark, the Epiphany hymn rings haste
From its loveliest biding-place

At the refectory of your loving-care
the transfiguration clarion sounds a call
that didactae could ne're convey nor spare.

Hark, the Epiphany hymn rings haste
From its loveliest biding-place

Thus, Gospel comes ensconced in Word and Deed
and the evidence is your shimmering touch:
Christus Victor, shown in a life's sown seed.

Hark, the Epiphany hymn rings haste
From its loveliest biding-place

❦ *Tristan Gylberd (1954–)* ❦

O Jesus, shine around us
With radiance of thy grace;
O Jesus, turn upon us
The brightness of thy face.
We need no star to guide us
As on our way we press,
If thou thy light vouchsafest,
O Sun of Righteousness.

William Walsham How (1823–1897)

God moves in a mysterious way,
His wonders to perform;
He plants his footsteps in the sea,
And rides upon the storm.

Ye fearful saints fresh courage take,
The clouds ye so much dread
Are big with mercy, and shall break
In blessings on your head.

Judge not the Lord by feeble sense,
But trust him for his grace;
Behind a frowning providence,
He hides a smiling face.

Blind unbelief is sure to err,
And scan his work in vain;
God is his own interpreter,
And he will make it plain.

William Cowper (1731–1800)

Epiphany Carols and Hymns

Sweet Flowerets of the Martyr Band
Salvete, flores martyrum
Aurelius Clemens Prudentius, c. 348–413
This hymn, by the Spanish poet Aurelius Clemens Prudentius, is part of a larger poem that is in turn part of a larger collection entitled *Cathermerinon.* This section was the first part of the work to find its way into general liturgical use by the Church, being found as early as the 11th-century. It is a remembrance of the first martyrs, the children whom Herod massacred in his attempt to kill the infant Christ. It is also a reminder that the actions of men are subject to the will of God—Herod could not stop the Savior's path. God's plans and purposes always prevail.

Sweet flowerets of the martyr band,
    Plucked by the tyrant's ruthless hand
Upon the threshold of the morn,
    Like rosebuds by a tempest torn;

First victims for the Incarnate Lord,
    A tender flock to feel the sword;
Beside the very altar, gay
    With palm and crown, ye seemed to play.

Ah! what availed king Herod's wrath?
    He could not stop the Saviour's path:

Alone, while others murdered lay,
    In safety Christ is borne away.

O Lord, the Virgin-born, to Thee
    Eternal praise and glory be,
Whom with the Father we adore
    And Holy Ghost for evermore.

A HYMN FOR MARTYRS SWEETLY SING
Hymnum canentes martyrum
The Venerable Bede, 673–735
Translated by Joan Mason Neale, 1818–1866
The Venerable Bede is best known as the historian of the Early English
Church. The following stanzas are the first, fourth, and sixth out of eight.
This too is a reminder of the slaughter of the Holy Innocents.

A Hymn for Martyrs sweetly sing;
    For Innocents your praises bring;
Of whom in tears was earth bereaved,
    Whom heaven with songs of joy received;
Whose Angels see the Father's face
    World without end, and hymn His grace;
And, while they praise their glorious King,
    A hymn for Martyrs sweetly sing.

A voice from Ramah was there sent,
    A voice of weeping and lament,

While Rachel mourned her children sore,
    Whom for the tyrant's sword she bore.
After brief taste of earthly woe
    Eternal triumph now they know;
For whom, by cruel torments rent,
    A voice from Ramah was there sent.

And every tear is wiped away
    By your dear Father's hands for aye:
Death hath no power to hurt you more;
    Your own is life's eternal shore.
And all who, good seed bearing, weep,
    In everlasting joy shall reap,
What time they shine in heavenly day,
    And every tear is wiped away.

THE COVENTRY CAROL
Anonymous, c. 14th century
This carol falls at the end of *The Pageant of the Shearman and Tailors*, one of a cycle of mystery plays that were performed in Coventry each year on the feast of Corpus Christi. The Medieval Mystery plays date from the 14th and 15th centuries and exist in the form of cycles of plays that tell the redemption story from the Fall of Man in the Garden of Eden to the Last Judgment. The purpose of these plays was didactic as they were based on Scripture. Each of the individual plays was financed and brought forth by one of the craft-guilds (or "mysteries") of the city in a vast processional production on carts that lasted from dawn until after midnight. Repeated thematic elements and rhyme schemes within and between the individual

plays unify the plays in each of the cycles. Cities famous for the play cycles included Coventry, York, Chester, and Wakefield. The plays at Coventry were first mentioned in 1392, but the earliest known manuscript is from a copy by Robart Croo from 14 March 1534. These plays were sponsored by Queen Margaret in 1456 and later by Henry VII in 1492. *The Pageant of the Shearman and Tailors* falls into two halves. The first part is introduced by Isaiah and covers the annunciation to Mary, the Nativity, and the annunciation to the shepherds. The second half contains the adoration of the three kings, the flight into Egypt, and the massacre of the Innocents. The directions for the following carol are as follows: "Here the Wemen cum in wythe there chyldur, syngyng to them; Mare and Joseff goth away clene. First Woman: I lull my chyld wondursly swete, And in my armis I do hyt kepe, Be-cawse thatt yt schuld not crye." Their singing is to put the children to sleep lest the soldiers of Herod locate them by their crying. The song comes as the emotional climax of a highly dramatic moment in the long play. The play ends when the soldiers report back to Herod.

Lully, lulla, thow littel tyne child,
By, by, lully, lulla, thow littel child,
By, by lully, lullay.

O sisters too, How may we do
    For to preserve this day
This poor yongling For whom we do sing:
    "By, by, lully, lullay"?

Herod the King In his raging
    Chargid he hath this day

His men of might In his owne sight
    All yonge children to slay.

That wo is me, Pore child, for thee,
    And ever morne and say
For thi parting Nether say nor singe:
    "By, by, lully, lullay."

EARTH HAS MANY A NOBLE CITY
O Sola Magnarum Urbium
Aurelius Clemens Prudentius, c. 348–413
Translated by Edward Caswall, 1814–1878
Although primarily known for *Of the Father's Love Begotten*, Aurelius
Clemens Prudentius' Epiphany poem *Earth Has Many a Noble City* is also
one of his best lyrics. These hymns are some of the oldest and most signifi-
cant carols written. Prudentius started writing poetry after giving up his
successful career as a lawyer and judge to withdraw to a monastery. It was
in the contemplative environment that he wrote his most enduring works
filled with allusion and theology.

Earth has many a noble city;
    Bethlehem, thou dost all excel:
Out of thee the Lord from heaven
    Came to rule His Israel.

Fairer than the sun at morning
    Was the star that told His birth,

To the world its God announcing
    Seen in fleshly form on earth.

Eastern sages at His cradle
    Make oblations rich and rare;
See them give, in deep devotion,
    Gold, and frankincense, and myrrh.

Sacred gifts of mystic meaning:
    Incense doth their God disclose,
Gold the King of kings proclaimeth,
    Myrrh His sepulchre foreshows.

Jesu, Whom the Gentiles worshipped
    At Thy glad Epiphany,
Unto Thee, with God the Father
    And the Spirit, glory be.

As With Gladness Men of Old
William Chatterton Dix, 1837–1898

When William Chatterton Dix was in his early twenties, he lay recovering from an illness. On January 6, he read the gospel lesson for the day that was the Epiphany story from Matthew 2:1–12. He was inspired by the lesson and wrote this hymn before evening. The strength of these words is manifest not only in the telling of the wise men's story but also in the application to the hearer. Dix enjoins the listener in prayer to be led to God, to seek the mercy seat, to bring costly treasures to Christ, and to find the entrance to Glory through the work of Christ. Although Dix worked in insurance, he still found opportunity to write hymns, including the Christmas favorite, *What Child is This.*

As with gladness men of old
    Did the guiding star behold;
As with joy they hailed its light,
    Leading onward, beaming bright;
So, most gracious God, may we
    Evermore be led to thee.

As with joyful steps they sped
    To that lowly manger bed,
There to bend the knee before
    Him who heaven and earth adore;
So may we with willing feet
    Ever seek thy mercy seat.

As they offered gifts most rare
    At that manger rude and bare;
So may we with holy joy,
    Pure and free from sin's alloy,
All our costliest treasures bring,
    Christ, to thee, our heavenly King.

Holy Jesus, every day
    Keep us in the narrow way;
And, when earthly things are past,
    Bring our ransomed souls at last
Where they need no star to guide,
    Where no clouds thy glory hide.

In the heavenly country bright
    Need they no created light;
Thou its light, its joy, its crown,
    Thou its sun which goes not down;
There for ever may we sing
    Alleluias to our King.

BRIGHTEST AND BEST OF THE SONS OF THE MORNING
Bishop Reginald Heber, 1783–1826
When Reginald Heber first published this carol in November of 1811, it
was regarded as bordering on star worship and too dance-like. Heber wrote
this carol on Epiphany Sunday in accordance with his principle that hymns
ought to be liturgical by following the Church year. It is based on the

gospel reading for that day (Matthew 2:1-12, The Wise Men seeking for the infant Christ) as well as Revelation 22:16 in which the Redeemer is also symbolized as the "bright and morning star." Heber, an Oxford educated Anglican cleric, was the vicar at the small village of Hodnet in Shropshire (1807–1822) before becoming the Bishop of Calcutta, India where he planted the gospel until his death in 1826. In addition to *Brightest and Best*, he is also well known for his hymns *The Son of God Goes Forth to War* and *Holy, Holy, Holy*.

Brightest and best of the sons of the morning,
    Dawn on our darkness, and lend us thine aid;
Star of the East, the horizon adorning,
    Guide where our infant Redeemer is laid.

Cold on His cradle the dewdrops are shining;
    Low lies His head with the beasts of the stall;
Angels adore Him in slumber reclining,
    Maker and Monarch and Saviour of all.

Shall we then yield Him, in costly devotion,
    Odors of Edom, and offerings divine,
Gems of the mountain, and pearls of the ocean,
    Myrrh from the forest, and gold from the mine?

Vainly we offer each ample oblation,
    Vainly with gifts would His favor secure;
Richer by far is the heart's adoration,
    Dearer to God are the prayers of the poor.

GOOD KING WENCESLAS
John Mason Neale, 1818–1866
John Mason Neale was the son of an Evangelical clergyman and was born in London. He had a distinguished career at Cambridge University. In addition to many hymns he wrote, Neale utilized his gift for Greek and Latin to translate many of the hymns of the Medieval Church. *O Come, O Come, Emmanuel* is among the finest of his efforts. *Good King Wenceslas* is one of his original works in which he sets to poetry one of the many Bohemian legends about Duke Wenceslas the Holy. Wenceslas ruled Bohemia between 928–935. He was renown for his kindness to the poor, especially at Christmas and on the Feast Day of St. Stephen the Martyr (December 26). This carol tells, in dialogue form, the story of Wenceslas and his page delivering food, drink, and firewood to a peasant's house in the dark and cold of winter. The carol ends with the admonition that men shall blessing for themselves by blessing the poor.

Good King Wenceslas looked out
   On the Feast of Stephen,
When the snow lay round about,
   Deep and crisp and even;
Brightly shone the moon that night,
   Though the frost was cruel,
When a poor man came in sight,
   Gathering winter fuel.

"Hither, page, and stand by me,
   If thou knowest it, telling;
Yonder peasant, who is he?

Where and what his dwelling?"
"Sire, he lives a good league hence,
    Underneath the mountain,
Right against the forest fence,
    By Saint Agnes' fountain."

"Bring me flesh, and bring me wine,
    Bring me pine logs hither;
Thou and I will see him dine
    When we bear them thither."
Page and monarch forth they went,
    Forth they went together;
Through the rude wind's wild lament
    And the bitter weather.

"Sire, the night is darker now,
    And the wind blows stronger;
Fails my heart, I know not how,
    I can go no longer."
"Mark my footsteps, my good page,
    Tread thou in them boldly;
Thou shalt find the winter's rage
    Freeze thy blood less coldly."

In his master's steps he trod,
    Where the snow lay dinted;
Heat was in the very sod
    Which the saint had printed.

Therefore, Christian men, be sure,
   Wealth or rank possessing,
Ye who now will bless the poor,
   Shall yourselves find blessing.

Epiphany Ballads and Verse

Miracles at the Birth of Christ
Isaac Watts, 1674–1748
Isaac Watts wrote over 750 hymns in his lifetime including versions of all one hundred and fifty psalms in rhyme. Although Watts was unable to serve his London Puritan congregation because of ill health, he remained active in the lives of the parishioners. His most famous Christmas poem is a poetic version of Psalm 98, *Joy to the World*.

The King of Glory sends his Son
    To make his entrance on this earth;
Behold the midnight bright as noon,
    And heavenly hosts declare his birth.

About the young Redeemer's head
    What wonders and what glories meet!
An unknown star arose, and led
    The eastern sages to his feet.

Simeon and Anna both conspire
    The infant-Saviour to proclaim;
Inward they felt the sacred fire,
    And blessed the babe, and owned his name.

Let Jews and Greeks blaspheme aloud,
    And treat the holy child with scorn;

Our souls adore the eternal God
    Who condescended to be born.

ST. STEPHEN AND KING HEROD
Anonymous
The feast day of St. Stephen the Martyr December 26th, and this close
proximity to the celebration of the birth of Christ, naturally led to a connection between Stephen and the Christmas story in this English ballad.

Saint Stephen was a clerk
    In King Herod's hall,
And servèd him of bread and cloth
    As every king befall.

Stephen out of kitchen came
    With boar's head on hand,
He saw a star was fair and bright
    Over Bethlehem stand.

He cast adown the boar's head
    And went into the hall;
"I forsake thee, Herod,
    And thy workès all.

"I forsake thee, King Herod,
    And thy workès all,
There is a child in Bethlehem born

Is better than we all."
"What aileth thee, Stephen?
   What is thee befall?
Lacketh thee either meat or drink
   In King Herod's hall?"

"Lacketh me neither meat or drink
   In King Herod's hall;
There is a child in Bethlehem born
   Is better than we all."

"What aileth thee Stephen?
   Art wode or 'ginnest to brede?
Lacketh thee either gold or fee,
   Or any rich weed?"

"Lacketh me neither gold ne fee
   Ne none rich weed;
There is a child in Bethlehem born
   Shall helpen us at our need."

"That is all so sooth, Stephen,
   All so sooth, I-wys,
As this capon crowè shall
   That li'th here in my dish."

That word was not so soon said,
   That word in that hall,

The capon crew Christus natus est
 Among the lordès all.
"Risit up, my tormentors,
 By two and all by one,
And leadit Stephen out of this town,
 And stonit him with stone."

Tooken they Stephen
 And stoned him in the way;
And therefore is his even
 On Christe's own day.

THE WISE MEN
G. K. Chesterton, 1874–1936

Gilbert Keith Chesterton was a man of extraordinary wit, intellect, and insight. He was a prolific writer who engaged the leading intellectuals of his time in debates, always defending the cause of orthodoxy. It was his good and affable nature that made his adversaries also his friends. Chesterton was a master of conveying truth through paradox, and this poignant and pointed poem is a fine example of his rare gifts.

Step softly, under snow or rain,
 To find the place where men can pray;
The way is all so very plain
That we may lose the way.

Oh, we have learnt to peer and pore
 On tortured puzzles from our youth,
We know all labyrinthine lore,

We are the three wise men of yore,
    And we know all things but the truth.

We have gone round and round the hill
    And lost the wood among the trees,
And learnt long names for every ill,
And served the mad gods, naming still
    The furies the Eumenides.

The gods of violence took the veil
    Of vision and philosophy,
The Serpent that brought all men bale,
He bites his own accursed tail,
    And calls himself Eternity.

Go humbly…it has hailed and snowed…
    With voices low and lanterns lit;
So very simple is the road,
    That we may stray from it.

The world grows terrible and white,
    And blinding white the breaking day;
We walk bewildered in the light,
For something is too large for sight,
    And something much too plain to say.

The Child that was ere worlds begun
    (…We need but walk a little way,
We need but see a latch undone…)

The Child that played with moon and sun
    Is playing with a little hay.

The house from which the heavens are fed,
    The old strange house that is our own,
Where trick of words are never said,
And Mercy is as plain as bread,
    And Honour is as hard as stone.

Go humbly, humble are the skies,
    And low and large and fierce the Star;
So very near the Manger lies
    That we may travel far.

Hark! Laughter like a lion wakes
    To roar to the resounding plain.
And the whole heaven shouts and shakes,
    For God Himself is born again,
And we are little children walking
    Through the snow and rain.

Prayers for Epiphany

Year's End
O Love beyond compare,
Thou art good when thou givest,
    when thou takest away,
    when the sun shines upon me,
    when night gathers over me.
Thou hast loved me before the foundation of the world,
and in love didst redeem my soul;
Thou dost love me still,
    in spite of my hard heart, ingratitude, distrust.
thy goodness has been with me during another year,
    leading me through a twisting wilderness,
    in retreat helping me to advance,
    when beaten back making sure headway.
Thy goodness will be with me in the year ahead;
I hoist sail and draw up anchor,
With thee as the blessed pilot of my future as of my past.
I bless thee that thou hast veiled my eyes to the waters ahead.
If thou hast appointed storms of tribulation,
    thou wilt be with me in them;
If I have to pass through tempests of persecution and temptation,
    I shall not drown;
If I am to die,
    I shall see thy face the sooner;
If a painful end is to be my lot,

grant me grace that my faith fail not;
If I am to be cast aside from the service I love,
   I can make no stipulation;
Only glorify thyself in me whether in comfort or trial,
   as a chosen vessel meet always for thy use.

PRAYER FOR THE NEW YEAR
O Lord,
Length of days does not profit me except the days are
   passed in thy presence,
   in thy service, to thy glory.
Give me a grace that precedes, follows, guides, sustains,
   sanctifies, aids every hour,
that I may not be one moment apart from thee,
but may rely on thy Spirit
   to supply every thought,
   speak in every word,
   direct every step,
   prosper every work,
   build up every mote of faith,
   and give me a desire
      to show forth thy praise,
      testify thy love,
      advance thy kingdom.
I launch my bark on the unknown waters of this year,
   with thee, O Father, as my harbour,
   thee, O Son, at my helm,
   thee, O Holy Spirit, filling my sails.

Guide me to heaven with my lamp burning,
     my ear open to thy calls,
     my heart full of love,
     my soul free,
Give me thy grace to sanctify me,
   thy comforts to cheer,
   thy wisdom to teach,
   thy right hand to guide,
   thy counsel to instruct,
   thy law to judge,
   thy presence to stabilize.
May thy fear by my awe,
   thy triumphs my joy. Amen.

THE PRAYER OF THE APPEARANCE
Luke 2:29-32
Lord, now You are letting
Your servant depart in peace,
According to Your Word;
For my eyes have seen Your salvation
Which You have prepared before the face of all peoples,
A light to bring revelation to the Gentiles,
And the glory of Your people, Israel.

PRAYER FOR EPIPHANY, JANUARY 6
Book of Common Prayer, 1789
O God,
 who by the leading of a star
   didst manifest thy only-begotten Son
   to the peoples of the earth:
Lead us, who know thee now by faith,
 to thy presence,
 where we may behold thy glory face to face;
through the same Jesus Christ our Lord,
 who liveth and reigneth with thee
 and the Holy Spirit,
 one God, now and for ever. *Amen.*

Daily Readings for Epiphany

December 26
The Feast day of St. Stephen the Martyr
Acts 6:1–15; 7:54–8:3 — The martyrdom of St. Stephen.

December 27
The Feast Day of St. John the Evangelist
Revelation 4:1-11 — St. John's vision of the throne of God.

December 28
The Holy Innocents
Matthew 2:16-18 — The slaughter of the Innocents.

December 29
1 John 1:1–2:6 — The true witness of the Light of God.

December 30
Isaiah 25:1-9 — The people have waited for the salvation of the Lord.

December 31
Isaiah 55 — Seek the Lord while he may be found.

January 1
The Circumcision of Christ
Luke 2:21-24 — The Circumcision of Christ.

JANUARY 2
Luke 2:25-35 — Simeon blesses the Christ child.

JANUARY 3
Luke 2:36-40 — Anna gives thanks for the redemption of Israel.

JANUARY 4
Matthew 2:1-8 — The wise men come from the East and meet with Herod.

JANUARY 5
Twelfth Night
Matthew 2:9-23 — The wise men present gifts to the Christ child and are warned of Herod's plot.

JANUARY 6
Epiphany
Isaiah 49:1-17 — The gift of the Saviour is for all people.

KING WENCESLAUS AND THE HAPPY APPEARANCE

The happy appearance of Christ in the world has made for a new dispensation of civic virtue. Because the Lord abides forever, He has established His Throne for judgment, and He will judge the world in righteousness. He will surely execute judgment for the peoples with equity. The Lord also will be a Stronghold for the oppressed, a Stronghold in times of trouble. As a consequence, a royal regent must needs be a bastion of both justice and mercy.

WENCESLAUS OF BOHEMIA (907–929)

The legendary generosity and charity of Good King Wenceslaus of Bohemia, is no mere Yuletide fable. The young prince lived a life fraught with conflict and tragedy. Both his mother and grandmother—victims of court intrigue and anti-Christian conspiracy—were murdered when he was young. He himself was the object of several assassination attempts and revolts. Yet, despite such adversity, he was a model Christian regent. He reformed the penal system. He criminalized abuse of children and outcasts. And he exercised great compassion on the poor.

His royal grandparents, Borivoy and his queen, Ludmila, were converted and baptized despite the strong opposition of a number of noble Czech families who wished to maintain their control over the Pagan cults. Borivoy and Ludmila had a son, Ratislav who ultimately ruled the realm in their stead—a compromise with those powerful families designed to preserve the tenuous peace. In time, he married Drahomira, daughter of the chief of the

Veletians, a Slav tribe from the north. Together, they had twin sons Wenceslaus and Boleslaus.

Wenceslaus was raised by his godly grandmother Ludmila while Boleslaus remained with his mother and father in the court. As a result, the future king was not only raised as a Christian, he was able to witness first hand the sacrifices believers had to undergo—apart from all the political intrigue of the royal court.

Wenceslaus was still young when his father died in battle. His mother Drahomira served as the regent for her sons. Alas, she was greatly influenced by the powerful pagan families still in Bohemia. She allowed a series of fiercely anti-Christian policies to be implemented throughout the land. During the persecutions that broke out, Ludmila was assassinated while she was praying. Though still just an adolescent, Wenceslaus found support from among the common people. After several months of struggle, Drahomira was driven out and Wenceslaus was made ruler. He straightway announced the initiation of Scriptural standards of justice and mercy— without prejudice—to all within the kingdom.

The little kingdom prospered under the young king's benevolent rule. At peace with their neighbors—Wenceslaus cultivated friendly relations with the Carolignian Empire by acknowledging Henry as the legitimate successor of Charlemagne in 926. The poor and the needy, the despised and the rejected were the special beneficiaries of the new found peace and prosperity.

Wenceslaus understood only too well that God is merciful and just. According to Scripture, He works righteousness and justice for all (Psalm 33:5). Morning by morning, He dispenses His justice without fail (Zephaniah 3:5) and without partiality (Job 32:21). All his ways are just

(Deuteronomy 32:4) so that injustice is an abomination to Him (Proverbs 11:1).

Thus, He is adamant about ensuring the cause of the meek and the weak (Psalm 103:6). Time after time, Scripture stresses this important truth. God cares for the needy. And His people are to do likewise.

God desires that His people follow Him (Matthew 4:19). We are to emulate Him (1 Peter 1:16). We are to do as He does. In effect, we are to do unto others as He has done unto us. That is the ethical principle that underlies the "Golden Rule" (Matthew 7:12; Luke 6:31).

If God has comforted us, then we are to comfort others (2 Corinthians 1:4). If God has forgiven us, then we are to forgive others (Ephesians 4:32). If God has loved us, then we are to love others (1 John 4:11). If He has taught us, then we are to teach others (Matthew 28:20). If He has borne witness to us, then we are to bear witness to others (John 15:26-27). If He has laid down His life for us, then we are to lay down our lives for one another (1 John 3:16).

Whenever God commanded the priestly nation of Israel to imitate Him in ensuring justice for the wandering homeless, the alien, and the sojourner, He reminded them that they were once despised, rejected, and homeless themselves (Exodus 22:21-27; 23:9; Leviticus 19:33-34). It was only by the grace and mercy of God that they had been redeemed from that low estate (Deuteronomy 24:17-22). Thus they were to exercise compassion to the broken-hearted and the dispossessed. They were to serve.

Priestly privilege brings priestly responsibility. If Israel refused to take up that responsibility then God would revoke their privilege (Isaiah 1:11-17). If they refused to exercise reciprocal mercy then God would rise up in His anger to visit the land with His wrath and displeasure, expelling them into the howling wilderness once again (Exodus 22:24). On the other hand, if they fulfilled their calling to live lives of merciful service then they would ever be blessed (Psalm 41:1-2).

The principle still holds true. Those of us who have received the compassion of the Lord on High are to demonstrate tenderness in kind to all those around us. This is precisely the lesson Jesus was driving at in the parable of the unmerciful slave: "For this reason the kingdom of heaven may be compared to a certain king who wished to settle accounts with his slaves. And when he had begun to settle them, there was brought to him one who owed him ten thousand talents. But since he did not have the means to repay, his lord commanded him to be sold, along with his wife and children and all that he had, and repayment to be made. The slave therefore falling down, prostrated himself before him, saying, 'Have patience with me, and I will repay you everything.' And the lord of that slave felt compassion and released him and forgave him the debt. But that slave went out and found one of his fellow slaves who owed him a hundred denarii; and he seized him and began to choke him, saying, 'Pay back what you owe.' So his fellow slave fell down and began to entreat him, saying, 'Have patience with me and I will repay you.' He was unwilling however, but went and threw him in prison until he should pay back what was owed. So when his fellow slaves saw what had happened, they were deeply grieved and came and reported to their lord all that had happened. Then summoning him, his lord said to him, 'You wicked slave, I forgave you all that debt because you entreated me. Should you not also have had mercy on your fellow slave, even as I had mercy on you?' And his lord, moved with anger, handed him over to the torturers until he should repay all that was owed him. So shall My heavenly Father also do to you, if each of you does not forgive his brother from your heart" (Matthew 18:23-35).

The moral of the parable is crystal clear. The needy around us are living symbols of our own former helplessness and privation. We are therefore to be living symbols of God's justice, mercy, and compassion. We are to do as He has done (John 15:1-8). God has set the pattern by His gracious working in our lives. Now we are to follow that pattern by serving others in the power of the indwelling Spirit (John 14:15-26).

In other words, the Gospel calls us to live daily as if people really matter. It calls us to live lives of selfless concern. We are to pay attention to the needs of others—in both word and deed, in both thought and action we are to weave ordinary kindness into the very fabric of our lives (Deuteronomy 22:4).

But this kind of ingrained mercy goes far beyond mere politeness. We are to demonstrate concern for the poor (Psalm 41:1). We are to show pity toward the weak (Psalm 72:13). We are to rescue the afflicted from violence (Psalm 72:14). We are to familiarize ourselves with the case of the helpless (Proverbs 29:7), give of our wealth (Deuteronomy 26:12-13), and share of our sustenance (Proverbs 22:9). We are to "put on tender mercies, kindness, humbleness of mind, meekness, and long-suffering" (Colossians 3:12). We are to become "a father to the poor," and to "search out the case of the stranger" (Job 29:16). We are to love our neighbors as ourselves (Mark 12:31) and "rescue the perishing" (Proverbs 24:10-12), thus "fulfilling the law" (Romans 13:10).

According to the Scriptures, this kind of comprehensive servanthood emphasis is in fact, a primary indication of the authenticity of our faith, "This is pure and undefiled religion in the sight of our God and Father, to visit the orphans and widows in their distress and to keep oneself unstained by the world" (James 1:27).

We are called to "do justice" and to "love kindness" (Genesis 18:19).

We are to be ministers of God's peace (Matthew 5:9), instruments of His love (John 13:35), and ambassadors of His Kingdom (2 Corinthians 5:20). We are to care for the helpless, feed the hungry (Ezekiel 18:7), clothe the naked (Luke 3:11), shelter the homeless (Isaiah 16:3-4), visit the prisoner (Matthew 25:36), and protect the innocent (Psalm 82:4). We are to live lives of merciful service.

Wenceslaus understood this. But he did more than just understand it theoretically, he applied it practically in the administration of his little realm. The result was that he was deeply loved by his subjects. Wherever he went within the borders of the land he was thronged by well wishers. Eventually, the young king married and had a young son. Alas, the acclaim and good fortune became a bit too much for his brother, Boleslaus, to bear. He became insanely jealous. And to make matters worse, Wenceslaus's son would now rule after the king died. That meant that Boleslaus would never have the chance to rule. Boleslaus decided to join the party of influential Pagan nobles that had formed against the crown.

Early one morning, as Wenceslaus made his way to church, he met his brother. Boleslaus struck Wenceslaus and they began to struggle. A number of the Pagan lords who accompanied Boleslaus ran up and killed Wenceslaus, who murmured as he fell at the chapel door, "Brother, may God forgive you."

The common people at once began to acclaim Wenceslaus a martyr. Miracles were even attributed to him. In time, Boleslaus, stricken with guilt and remorse, repented of his terrible deed and had his brother's body translated to the church of St. Vitus at Prague three years after his death. The shrine quickly became a place of pilgrimage.

Amazingly, Wenceslaus by his death did what he was unable to do while he was living—he not only ensured the complete conversion of Bohemia, he was able to codify his deeds of mercy as a standard for Christian civic justice and mercy. By the beginning of the eleventh century Wenceslaus was already regarded as the patron of both the Czechs and the Slovaks. And his example became the pattern for living in light of the Epiphany of Christ in the midst of this poor fallen world.

Epiphany Traditions

St. Stephen's Day

Like Wenceslaus, Stephen (c. 35) was killed because of his convictions about the revelation of Christ in the world. Indeed, according to the Book of Acts, he was the very first martyr of the Christian faith. For centuries, Christians have remembered his faithfulness on the day after Christmas, December 26. It is a day for selfless care for the needy, the despised, and the unloved.

Boxing Day

December 26 is also commemorated as an official holiday in Britain known as Boxing Day. On this day boxes of food are to be delivered to the needy, and in days gone by were given to servants from their employers. The spirit of Wenceslaus is demonstrated so that the entire community may celebrate with joy the manifestation of the Good News. Often churches organize the day to particularly serve the physical and spiritual needs of their neighbors and thus demonstrate that the Scriptural injunctions to exercise Word and Deed compassion are still in full force.

St. John's Day

John, the beloved Apostle, was one of the founders of the church in Ephesus. He carried out his pastoral charge with particular compassion to the hurting and forlorn. As a result, his testimony has long been commemorated during this season of practical charity. It is on December 27 that the winter beers are uncasked, distributed to the poor, and that the dark is drawn for the blessing and benefit of all the townspeople and those who live beyond in field and forest.

FEAST OF THE HOLY INNOCENTS

Often called Childermas, the Feast of the Holy Innocents solemnizes the slaughter of the children of Judea by Herod the Great following the birth of Christ. It has always been the focus of the Christian's commitment to protect and preserve the sanctity of human life—thus serving as a prophetic warning against the practitioners of abandonment and infanticide in the age of antiquity, oblacy and pessiary in the medieval epoch, and abortion and euthanasia in these modern times. Generally set aside as a day of prayer, it culminates with a declaration of the covenant community's unflinching commitment to the innocents who are unable to protect themselves.

NEW YEARS DAY

Throughout Christendom, January 1 has been celebrated as a day of renewal—for vows, vision, and vocation. It was on this day that guild members took their annual pledge, that husbands and wives renewed their marriage promises, and that young believers reasserted their resolution to walk in the grace of the Lord's great Epiphany. In Edinburgh beginning in the seventeenth century, revelers would gather at the Tron Church to watch the great clock tower mark their entrance into the new year—which was the inspiration behind the relatively recent Times Square ceremony in New York. But in Edinburgh, the purpose was not merely to have a grand excuse for a public party, but a way of celebrating the truth of Epiphany newness.

THE TWELVE DAYS OF CHRISTMAS

Every day, from December 25 to January 6, was traditionally a part of the Yuletide celebration. Dedicated to mercy and compassion—in light of the incarnation of Heaven's own mercy and compassion—each of those twelve days between Christmas and Epiphany was to be noted by selfless giving and tender charity. In many cultures, gift giving is not concentrated on a single day, but rather, as in the famous folk song, spread out through the entire season.

A PARTRIDGE IN A PEAR TREE

All of the gifts in the folk song Twelve Days of Christmas represent some aspect of the blessing of Christ's appearing. They portray the abundant life, the riches of the Christian inheritance, and the ultimate promise of heaven. They also depict the essential covenantal nature of life lived in community and accountability.

Treats for Epiphany

Irish Soda Bread

1½	cups all-purpose flour
1	cup whole wheat flour
1	teaspoon baking soda
½	teaspoon salt
¼	cup currants
1¼	to 1½ cups buttermilk
1	tablespoon butter, melted

Grease a baking sheet. In a large bowl combine the flour, baking soda, and salt. Stir in the currants. Add 1¼ cups of buttermilk and stir just until the dry ingredients are moistened. (Add more buttermilk, if necessary, to make a soft dough.) Turn the dough onto a lightly floured surface and knead gently for 1 to 2 minutes. Shape into a ball and place on a greased baking sheet. Pat into an 8-inch circle. Using a sharp knife or razor blade, cut a ½-inch deep X in the top of the dough. Bake at 425° for about 45 minutes or until golden.

Transfer to a wire rack, and brush with melted butter. Serve hot or at room temperature.

Makes 1 loaf.

Bubble and Squeak

1	medium onion, chopped
3	tablespoons bacon drippings (or butter)
2½	cups cooked shredded cabbage
2	cups mashed potatoes
1	cup chopped leftover cooked beef (or corned beef)
½	teaspoon salt
	Freshly ground black pepper to taste
	Wow-wow Sauce (recipe follows)

In a 10-inch skillet heat the bacon drippings and sauté the onion over medium heat for about 5 minutes or until soft. Place the cabbage in a colander and press to remove the excess liquid. Add the cabbage to the onions and stir in the potatoes. Cook, stirring frequently, for about 5 minutes or until the vegetables begin to brown. Stir in the meat, and season with salt and pepper. Continue cooking without stirring for about 10 minutes or until golden on bottom.

Invert the mixture onto a large serving plate. Cover with foil and keep warm in a 225° oven while preparing the Wow-Wow Sauce. Cut into wedges and serve with sauce.

Makes 6 servings.

Wow-Wow Sauce

2	tablespoons butter
2	tablespoons minced onion
2	tablespoons all-purpose flour
1	cup beef broth
1	tablespoon white wine vinegar
I	tablespoon Worcestershire sauce
1	tablespoon English-style mustard
½	teaspoon prepared horseradish
	Salt and freshly ground black pepper to taste
2	tablespoons finely chopped fresh parsley

In a 1½-quart saucepan melt the butter over medium heat and sauté the onion, stirring constantly, for about 3 minutes or until the onion is soft but not browned. Stir in the flour and cook for 1 minute, stirring constantly. Add the broth all at once and whisk until smooth. Stir in all of the remaining ingredients except the parsley. Bring to a boil. Reduce the heat to medium-low and simmer, stirring frequently, for about 10 minutes, until the sauce is thickened. Stir in the parsley.

Makes 6 servings.

Mince Pies

8   teaspoons butter, softened
       Short-crust pastry
1½   cups Mincemeat (recipe follows)

Preheat the oven to 375°. Butter the bottom and sides of eight 2½-inch tart tins with the softened butter, allowing 1 teaspoon of butter for each tin.

On a lightly floured surface, roll out the pastry into a circle about ⅛-inch thick. With a cookie cutter or the rim of a glass, cut sixteen 3 ½-inch rounds of pastry. Gently press 8 of the rounds, 1 at a time, into the tart tins. Then spoon about 3 tablespoons of mincemeat into each pastry shell. Dampen the outside edges of the pastry shells with water and carefully fit the remaining 8 rounds over them. Crimp the edges of the pastry together with fingers or the tines of a fork. Trim the excess pastry from around the rims with a sharp knife, and cut 2 small slits about ¼ inch apart in the top of each of the pies. Arrange the pies on a large baking sheet. Bake at 375° in the middle of the oven for 10 minutes. Reduce the heat to 350° and bake for 20 minutes longer or until the crust is golden brown. Run the blade of a knife around the inside edges of the pies to loosen them slightly, and set them aside to cool in the pans. Turn out the pies with a narrow spatula and serve.

Makes 8 individual pies.

Mincemeat

½	pound fresh beef suet, finely chopped
4	cups seedless raisins
2	cups dried currants
1	cup coarsely chopped almonds
½	cup coarsely chopped candied citron
½	cup coarsely chopped dried figs
½	cup coarsely chopped candied orange peel
¼	cup coarsely chopped lemon peel
4	cups peeled, cored, and coarsely chopped Granny Smith apples
1¼	cups sugar
1	teaspoon grated nutmeg
1	teaspoon ground allspice
1	teaspoon ground cinnamon
½	teaspoon ground cloves
2½	cups brandy
1	cup pale dry sherry

In a large bowl combine the suet, raisins, currants, almonds, citron, dried figs, candied orange peel, candied lemon peel, apples, sugar, nutmeg, allspice, cinnamon, and cloves, and mix thoroughly. Pour in the brandy and sherry, and mix with a large wooden spoon until all the ingredients are well moistened. Cover the bowl and set the mincemeat aside in a cool place (not the refrigerator) for at least 3 weeks.

Check the mincemeat once a week. As the liquid is absorbed by the fruit, replenish it with sherry and brandy, using about ¼ cup at a time.

Mincemeat can be kept indefinitely in a covered container in a cool place, without refrigeration, but after a month or so refrigerate it if desired.

Makes about 3 quarts.

Quick English Trifle

1	purchased pound cake or spongecake
⅓	cup apricot jam
⅓	cup raspberry or blackberry jam
6	almond macaroons, crumbled
8	zwieback biscuits, crumbled
⅓	cup Sherry
¼	cup Brandy

For the custard:

2	cups whole milk
¼	cup sugar, infused with vanilla (or ¼ cup sugar and ¼ teaspoon vanilla extract)
4	large eggs
¼	teaspoon salt
1	cup heavy cream
¼	cup toasted almonds

Halve the cake horizontally, then halve each half vertically. Put apricot jam in between two horizontal halves and raspberry jam betwen other two halves. Cut the cakes into ½ inch fingers and line the sides of a glass trifle bowl with alternating flavors of cake fingers.

In a separate bowl crumble the remaining fingers. Add the macaroons, crumbled zwieback, Sherry, and Brandy. Put the mixture in the middle of the trifle bowl. Cover and refrigerate.

In a saucepan heat the milk with the sugar until just scalded. Cool a little then add the eggs, salt, and heavy cream. Stir over low heat until thickened. Do not let it boil. Take off the heat and add vanilla if not added to sugar earlier.

Pour the custard mixture over the cake mixture in the bowl, cover, and return to the refrigerator to chill, preferably overnight for best taste.

Before serving, whip the cream with a little confectioner's sugar and pipe onto the trifle. Decorate with almonds and candied fruit if desired.

Makes 8 servings.

INDEX OF NAMES

SUBJECT INDEX